Engage

Engage

A Theological Field Education Toolkit

Edited by Matthew Floding

Foreword by Lucinda Huffaker

ROWMAN & LITTLEFIELD
Lanham • Boulder • New York • London

Published by Rowman & Littlefield
A wholly owned subsidiary of
The Rowman & Littlefield Publishing Group, Inc.
4501 Forbes Boulevard, Suite 200, Lanham, Maryland 20706
https://rowman.com

Unit A, Whitacre Mews, 26-34 Stannary Street, London SE11 4AB,
United Kingdom

Diagrams in chapter 2 provided by Ashlee Floding

British Library Cataloguing in Publication Information Available

Library of Congress Cataloging-in-Publication Data

Names: Floding, Matthew, 1955– editor.
Title: Engage : a theological field education toolkit / edited by Matthew Floding ; fore-
    word by Lucinda Huffaker.
Description: Lanham : Rowman & Littlefield, 2017. | Includes bibliographical references
    and index.
Identifiers: LCCN 2016041395 (print) | LCCN 2016047558 (ebook) | ISBN
    9781442273498 (cloth : alk. paper) | ISBN 9781442273504 (pbk. : alk. paper) | ISBN
    9781442273511 (electronic)
Subjects: LCSH: Pastoral theology—Fieldwork. | Clergy—Training of.
Classification: LCC BV4164.5 .E54 2017 (print) | LCC BV4164.5 (ebook) | DDC
    253.071/55—dc23
LC record available at https://lccn.loc.gov/2016041395

♾ ™ The paper used in this publication meets the minimum requirements of American
National Standard for Information Sciences Permanence of Paper for Printed Library
Materials, ANSI/NISO Z39.48-1992.

Printed in the United States of America

Contents

Foreword

Lucinda Huffaker

When I meet with students who are making plans for their theological field education, I find myself tempted to break into cheerleading for the type of educational experience upon which they are about to embark. Theological field education is uniquely situated at the intersection of theory and practice, an incubator for practical or embodied wisdom and a greenhouse for the cultivation of pastoral imagination. "Wake up!" I want to warn them. "Don't treat this as another box to check off in your graduation requirements! Don't think of this as your part-time job! Take this seriously! Experiential education is transformative! Open yourself—open yourself to be 'shaped by God and God's people'[1] at this critical point in your seminary education!"

Why am I inclined toward advocacy for my area of academic work? The first sentence of *Christian Practical Wisdom* says it with quiet profundity: practical wisdom is "the least understood, the hardest to learn, and often the most devalued kind of knowledge."[2] I have been occupied and preoccupied with teaching and learning issues for many years, and I know this trinitarian resistance runs very deep. Learning from experience is extremely difficult work. Because it is not well understood and takes time and skill to reflect on what and why we practice, we are not encouraged to do so.[3]

Fortunately, most of my students embrace their field education opportunities enthusiastically, along with a healthy dose of trepidation. Some feel they have come home to a familiar way of learning through apprenticeship, while others struggle with the shift to greater accountability for their own learning, and still others struggle to identify as learning something that is so different from their classroom experience. Theological field education *is* a different way to learn. It develops different skills of self-expression, emotional intelligence, and interpersonal attunement, of working through conflict and creating with others. Like someone starting a new exercise program, students will develop different sets of "muscles" by engaging their contexts and each other through practice and experience.

One reason *Engage: A Theological Field Education Toolkit* will be useful to readers is that these authors have wrestled with the pedagogical issues that accompany learning through practice. The authors have written their chapters as testimonials about transformative learning in ways that capture their own passionate engagement with students doing this work. These are practical suggestions offered by writers embodying their *own* practical wisdom about how they help students learn from theological field education!

Probably my most immediate association with "engage" comes from popular culture. One of the best known catchphrases of *Star Trek: The Next Generation* is "Engage!," which is how Captain Jean-Luc Picard orders his spaceship into action. For me, in this context it means "Let's go! Run the race. Take it on. Head into the wind. Embrace your learning, full-heartedly! *Engage* your field education—and be formed and transformed for God's work in the world."

Acknowledgments

I am grateful to be part of a generous and generative community called theological field educators. It is also an active community of practice. We work hard and have fun sharing our learning, telling our stories, and encouraging each other. That is how I have experienced the Association for Theological Field Education (ATFE) and in particular the Presbyterian/Reformed Theological Field Educators' caucus. The fruit of that connection, collaboration, and community in ATFE is at the heart of many of the chapters in this book. I offer heartfelt thanks for each of your contributions. I am indebted to you and continue to learn from you.

The format of this book and the shape of the chapters—intentionally inviting deep conversation between author, student, and supervisor-mentor—is inspired by the structure and dynamic of the field education program here at Duke Divinity School. I am particularly grateful for the faithful and fruitful conversations with my colleagues Rhonda Parker and Daniel Corpening.

Field educators are also close colleagues with all who seek to see the church flourish. It is our pleasure and privilege to work both sides of the crosswalk between classroom and context. We love and respect our academic partners within seminaries and divinity schools. At the same time we have similar admiration and respect for those ministerial leaders who are our partners in formation for ministry through supervision and mentoring of students. I wish to especially thank the academic theologians willing to use the crosswalk and contribute to this book.

Justin Ashworth deserves a word of thanks for formatting the document in timely fashion and for catching errant words and phrases with his academically trained eye. Sarah Stanton, acquisitions editor at Rowman & Littlefield, was particularly helpful at the conception stage of the book.

In theological field education students regularly hear our pedagogical refrain: action—reflection—action. Thank-you Marcia Lynn, Geoffrey John Robert, Kathryn Erin, and Margrethe Anne, for being the family laboratory in which that pedagogy is experienced in love.

Introduction

Matthew Floding

I firmly believe that engagement is a key to your formation for ministry during your seminary experience. Certainly that's true of the academic content: your level of mastery and the degree to which you invite its mastery of you. Field education invites you to bring the lectures in theology and biblical studies and the best of preaching and pastoral care textbooks into the pulpit and the hospital room and give them life in *your* practice of ministry. Then you reflect on your practice theologically with the help of veteran clergy and laypersons who are passionately committed to your formation. Repeat!

Picture a crosswalk. Traveling back and forth across the crosswalk between classroom and context will call for the deepest engagement you *cannot* yet imagine. How could you? We don't know what we don't know. But do know this: If you bring all that you are and all that you are learning and commit to engage deeply with yourself, your supervisor-mentor, the context itself, and the arts of ministry, you will experience, as a gift of grace, formation for faithful and authentic ministry with integrity. My field education colleagues and I witness this transformation year after year.

Imagine yourself crossing over to a new ministry context for the first time. You feel vulnerable! You recall the angel's words repeated throughout scripture, "Do not be afraid." So you take the risk and it starts out a bit awkwardly, this dance between two strangers. You're eager to engage in the practice of ministry, and the congregation (or nonprofit) and the pastor (or director) are eager to affirm their call to participate in your formation as a ministerial leader. Where do you begin? Which dance partner takes the lead? You both do!

Engage: A Theological Field Education Toolkit equips both you and your supervisor-mentor to engage this important relationship with energy and imagination. This book is not an introduction to ministry. Kathleen A. Cahalan's *Introducing the Practice of Ministry*; Christie Cozad Neuger's *The Arts of Ministry: Feminist-Womanist Approaches*; Ronald Edward Peters and Marsha Snulligan Haney's *Africentric Approaches to Christian Ministry: Strengthening Urban Congregations in African American Communities*; and William Willimon's *Pastor: The Theology and Practice of Ordained Ministry* (rev. ed.) are each helpful introductions.

Engage: A Theological Field Education Toolkit has a different and complementary focus. *Engage prepares you for the formational work of integrating the theory into your person through its actual practice*. This is seminary education at its best: engagement "nurturing embodied, situated knowing-in-action [that] . . . emerges in the interplay of various realms of knowing, from the most abstract generalized theories to the most concrete, practical situations."[1] In each chapter Christian scholars and practitioners imagine the challenging learning curve you face, recall their own learning and missteps, and give you their best guidance. Directly to you.

As a group the authors represent a diversity of denominational affiliations and type of institutions served. You will *experience* the voice and passion of each author. There has been no effort to disguise or edit the book in such a way that all of the authors write with the same voice. Professor Jason Byassee sounds like the passionate Duke basketball–loving United Methodist North Carolinian that he is. Professor John Stackhouse sounds like the hockey-loving Canadian Evangelical who can recall his roots in England that he is. As you read I hope you find that this approach gives the book added character. I am extremely grateful to each author for his or her contribution. It has been a delight to learn from each one. More important, I think you will enjoy reading each author's contribution because you sense that each cares deeply about the flourishing of the Church and about you and your formation for ministry. Every one of us does.

Your field education director will employ this book in a way that fits within your seminary's curriculum and field education program. You might find it especially useful as you prepare to engage in a placement to work through the foundational chapters, 1–8. By reading and then discussing chapters 2 and 3 with your supervisor-mentor soon after you begin your field education placement, you can establish common ground and an appreciation for each other's role in that relationship. As you engage within your context and prepare to design a learning-serving covenant, you might choose to focus on chapters 9–16, which speak directly to your ministerial arts focus. In peer reflection group you might discuss with one another some of the cultural and personal issues that impact your experience in ministry, covered in chapters 17–19. These chapters address the important topics of generational difference, gender, and race. In addition, most field education programs offer experiences outside of congregational settings. Chapters 20–24 prepare you to engage more deeply through technology and in nonprofit settings, clinical pastoral education (CPE), secular environments, and international opportunities.

What you are about to experience is called *theological field education*. No seminary experience is complete without it. Use the crosswalk. Engage your field education opportunity and you will find in it an inescapably theological and formational experience.

Chapter One

Engaging Theological Field Education

Matthew Floding

Field education is an opportunity for you to develop ministry skills, practice ministerial reflection, discern your call, experience professional collegiality, and undergo personal transformation. Your seminary or divinity school values students actually doing ministry so that you can integrate ministry theory and practice into who you are.

One image that is helpful to me is a crosswalk. I recall my own seminary experience as an intern at a suburban Chicago Presbyterian church. Each week I experienced moving back and forth across this crosswalk. I would cross from seminary, where we engaged scripture, theories of ministry, and theology, to my internship in the congregation. They were patient. Some weeks I'm sure my camp and campus ministry–fueled faith at best awkwardly incorporated what I was learning at seminary. It couldn't have been pretty. But they kept encouraging me. So I practiced and then my supervisor-mentor and I would sit down at our specified time and reflect together. Wise laypersons offered honest feedback and support. Their intentionality increased my love and passion for both: participating in the ministry of the Triune God of grace in their midst and the love of learning. Then I found myself moving back across the crosswalk to seminary energized and making connections. I learned to ask better questions. I was being formed in faith and formed for ministry.

The point here is that *you* will be traveling back and forth across the crosswalk. Seminary and ministry placement will inform each other as they are integrated into your person and will continue to do so throughout your life in ministry. No matter what ministry God is calling you to, field education will be a significant part of your preparation.

A LITTLE HISTORY

Today every Association of Theological Schools (ATS)–accredited theological seminary or divinity school in the United States and Canada provides field education.[1] This has not always been the case. I recall some years ago speaking with Pastor John Smith, who graduated from seminary in 1952. Back then, during the school year students initiated their own experience by volunteering at a local congregation to teach, preach, and assist the pastor. In the summer students sought paying summer assignments to broaden their experience. One summer John, the soon-to-be pastor, ministered in rural South Dakota. Since he didn't have a car, he hitchhiked to each of his pastoral call destinations! He was paid $15 per week. It was an amazing experience, even call-defining for him. In fact, he went on to a forty-year-plus ministry in rural churches. Students received no academic credit for their ministry, just experience and a modest paycheck. These experiences were often referred to as "fieldwork."

Seminary faculty, in the late 1950s and early 1960s, took note that students like John Smith entered the classroom energized by their experience and asked good questions informed by those experiences. Some faculty seized upon the opportunity to weave these experiences into the classroom and later into the curriculum as "field education." This move formally acknowledged that growth through practicing ministry was not simply work, but educational.

Impetus for further integrating field education into seminary curricula throughout North America came in 1966 as a result of a study, "Education for Ministry,"[2] sponsored by ATS and conducted by Charles Feilding, a professor of pastoral theology at Trinity College, Toronto. Feilding noted: "The trouble in the practical departments is the widespread tendency to replace practice with lectures about practice."[3] He went on to argue that an organized field education program was essential for theological education, for "nothing short of this can be taken seriously as professional education."[4] After the publication of "Education for Ministry," seminaries and divinity schools began to require students to engage in field education that included theological reflection on the practice of ministry with supervisor-mentors and peers.

YOUR GROWTH AND TRANSFORMATION

You'll be investing significant personal resources and three or more years of time in preparation for your calling. What are some of the factors you might consider as you enter this transforming educational process? You come from a rich and interesting matrix of family, educational, personal growth, and ministry experiences. It's good to acknowledge and be aware of the formation that has already taken place. God has already invested a great deal in your life! In the midst of all of this, God "spoke" to you in a way that led you to seminary. As you listen to your fellow students you will learn that each has a unique story to tell related to this matter of call. Don't feel overly anxious if you aren't certain at the beginning of your seminary experience about what God has in mind for you. Here's one thing you can count on: God seems pleased to use the process of seminary, and field education in particular, to clarify students' sense of call. This is what students report in self-evaluations as they reflect on their field education experience. For example, here "Stephen" reflects on an experience in his self-evaluation after his first semester of field education:

> One moment this semester that I felt particularly accompanied by God's presence occurred while teaching an adult education class. Following a showing of an International Justice Mission film on modern-day slavery, I explored their questions. I responded to one question with an explanation that our calling is to witness to the Kingdom of God. Though we cannot make God's Kingdom come, we do pray for it and act in ways that affirm how it will someday be. While "proclaiming" this good news, I felt a sense of energy and peace. While I judge myself to be a better writer than speaker, I believe the Spirit is building confidence in my speaking abilities.

For most students, entering seminary is a new beginning, and many feel a bit displaced. You may have moved across the country to attend a denominational seminary or a divinity school whose ethos was attractive to you. Perhaps you have left a career, and you and your family feel a bit like Abraham and Sarah going to a place that you've never been before. Nevertheless, you can be confident that God the caller, as with Sarah and Abraham, will lead to the place: "I will show you" (Gen. 12:1).

Perhaps an insight from the work of Erik Erikson will also encourage you. Recall Erikson's psychosocial theory from your general psychology class.[5] In his schema, we negotiate different challenges at each of the stages of development, paying special attention to social cues as we grow. When we enter a new experience, especially a new community, we—in a sense—renegotiate the earlier stages. For example, when you first entered the seminary environment and met your seminary colleagues, perhaps at an orientation, you first needed to establish whether you could trust (versus mistrust) this environment. If you determined you could, you ventured further, disclosing more of your ideas and feelings and gauging your peers' and professors' responses (initiative versus guilt). According to Erikson, we then move on to the adolescent stage, when we must negotiate "identity versus role confusion." Finding your place by moving through these stages will hopefully take you from feeling displaced to thinking, "I love my seminary community!"

Erikson's insights also inform how field education might help you understand the contours of your call. Social feedback is an important facet of field education. Field education provides hospitable ministry environments in which you will be encouraged to "try on" various ministry roles so that you can practice ministry, receive helpful feedback, and enjoy spaces to reflect on your experience. You will discover your ministry identity by doing ministry. Remember it is you, all that you are by nature and by grace, whom God is calling to ministry. This is illustrated well in a Hasidic tale.[6] When he was an old man, Rabbi Zusya said, "In the coming world, they will not ask me: 'Why were you not Moses?' They will ask me: 'Why were you not Zusya?'"

Field education also allows you to make adjustments to your mental "map" of the world. Your family of origin, education, religious and other life experiences, as well as regional and larger cultural forces have shaped your way of looking at the world. From all of these experiences you have formed an internal "map" of how the world works and how best to navigate it.[7] This map allows you to make sense of things and at times cope with extra-challenging experiences. Everyone else has formed a "map" too, and in seminary you will learn that each of our maps is a bit different and that given our cognitive limits, no one of us has the perfect "map." Some differences will appear in the classroom, some in your ministry settings, others elsewhere. Often you will feel uncomfortable, perhaps even disturbed, about these differences. You might feel your lack of ease with a situation even before you can name it. It is a ministerial skill to understand, even appreciate, another's way of framing the world in which he or she participates. Can you be flexible and patient enough to discern another's perspective? If you enter your field education placement with a spirit of generosity and as a learner, you will be richer for it and will learn to appreciate the strength in diversity of perspectives.

PLACE AND SPACE

The field education director at your theological school has cultivated a network of placement sites. You may enter a congregation or nonprofit that has recently adopted this role or a congregation whose identity has been connected to the seminary since its founding. Each of these settings takes its role with utmost seriousness and is working to be the best learning environment it can be. The members of a congregation understand full well that the leader they are training might someday be their own minister!

Field education is not a one-size-fits-all proposition. Your sense of call may be directing you toward a noncongregational setting. Your field education program has sites that allow students to explore call outside the walls of the congregation. Hospitals, prisons, campus ministries, community gardens, assisted living communities, restorative justice programs, and a myriad of other nonprofit settings may be options for you. You might consider engaging in an alternative context just to stretch your vision of ministry.

Supervisor-mentors have been oriented to the field education program and receive training to grow in their supervision skills. You soon will enter a hospitable place to practice ministry and will serve alongside a skilled supervisor-mentor. This place to practice ministry and space to reflect on it is where the experiential component of formation for ministry can flower. In the early part of the twentieth century one of the parents of adult education theory, Eduard Lindeman at Columbia University, wrote that "the resource of highest value in adult education is the learner's experience."[8] Raw experience doesn't guarantee that you or I will learn. In a delightful essay Joseph Levine, an education professor at Michigan State University, observes:

> Recently someone suggested to me that we learn more from our mistakes than our successes. How does that person know? I can think of lots of times when I haven't learned from either! . . . The key is that we have the power to learn from our mistakes. And the way we exercise this power is by taking time to reflect.[9]

Lindeman and Levine underscore the two most important components of learning in your ministry context: experience in the practice of ministry and reflection on that practice. Sometimes this is referred to as the action-reflection model of learning.[10] Your active participation in ministry will provide plenty of data for reflection, hopefully with many stories of effectiveness! But when mistakes happen—they surely will—and you have time to reflect on what took place and what happened within you, you can follow Levine's sage advice: "Reflection takes on its most powerful form when we're able to 'return to the scene of the crime' and act again. This suggests that to really learn from a mistake takes not only time to reflect but also the opportunity to try out the results of our reflection."[11] Through ministerial reflection in regular meetings with your supervisor-mentor, you will be able to reflect on your experience—successes and not so successful experiences—and turn these into powerful growth opportunities. Your supervisor-mentor has been trained in methods of ministerial reflection, and you will also receive training in ministerial reflection methods.[12] You may also have a lay mentoring team that is praying for you and will meet regularly with you to reflect on these experiences, and some members will share their skills by ministering alongside you.[13] Field education programs also provide peer reflection groups in which to process your ministry experiences using a variety of tools. Be alert to all of the wonderful resource persons God may use in your formation for ministry.

God has staked a claim in our formation experience. The psalmist confesses with wonder,

> For it was you who formed my inward parts;
>   You knit me together in my mother's womb.
> I praise you for I am fearfully and wonderfully made. (Ps. 139:13–14a)

The psalmist speaks of "being made in secret" (v. 15). Our formation, from creation to our life's end, is a work of grace that God has initiated by the Spirit. There is something deep and even mysterious going on in formation for ministry. Field education can empower you to discover who you are and give you and others glimpses of who you may become. Can you be open to God's surprises through your field education experience?

Perhaps this prayer of St. Brendan, which has been helpful to me, will be for you also:

> Help me to journey beyond the familiar and into the unknown.
> Give me the faith to leave old ways and break fresh ground with you.
> Christ of the mysteries,
> I trust you to be stronger than each storm within me.
> I will trust in the darkness and know that my times, even now, are in your hand.
> Tune my spirit to the music of heaven, and somehow, make my obedience count for you.
> Amen.[14]

QUESTIONS FOR REFLECTION

1. What biblical character's story of call reflects something of my own?
2. What is producing anxiety in me right now as I enter a field education placement?

SUGGESTED READING

Hamman, Jaco J. *Becoming a Pastor: Forming Self and Soul for Ministry*. Rev. ed. Cleveland, OH: Pilgrim Press, 2014.
Kincaid, William B. *Finding Voice: How Theological Field Education Shapes Pastoral Identity*. Eugene, OR: Wipf and Stock, 2012.
Palmer, Parker J. *Let Your Life Speak*. San Francisco: Jossey-Bass, 2000.

Chapter Two

Engaging with Your Supervisor-Mentor

Matthew Floding

Your supervisor-mentor is eager to meet you.[1] The training she received at your seminary or divinity school confirmed for her that to supervise and to mentor is a calling. She can't wait to begin, but may be a bit anxious. She knows the relationship with you is nothing short of a sacred trust.

How can you make the most of this relationship? Let's start by looking at assumptions your supervisor-mentor has about you.

WHAT YOUR SUPERVISOR-MENTOR ASSUMES ABOUT YOU

First, he believes you are motivated to practice the arts of ministry. Your supervisor-mentor views the opportunity you have to journey over a cross-walk from classroom to congregation as a holy pilgrimage that transforms. Since ministry is an embodied experience, he understands that it takes lots of practice, like learning to shoot a three-pointer consistently in basketball. Ministry is a whole-person experience. Your supervisor-mentor, from experience, knows that confirmation of call, integration of theory and practice, deep personal growth, and nurturing pastoral imagination are part of this internship.

Second, in her equipping as a supervisor-mentor, the learning theory that she has been introduced to has provided her with a set of expectations about the way that you will learn best in a field education opportunity.[2] The supervisor-mentor

- respects your agency in the learning process. She expects you to be eager to develop a focused, learning-serving covenant,[3] to take initiative in pursuing your learning goals, and to participate meaningfully in the evaluation process.

- accepts the responsibility to open doors of opportunity for you to practice the ministerial arts as a cornerstone for learning. She will assure a wide range of experiences as well as sustained engagement in your learning-serving covenant focus.
- affirms that there is an element of relevance in experiential learning. She understands, for example, that if you are taking a class in pastoral care, prioritizing visits to the hospital and to hospice is integral to your formation.
- expects the congregation to have an active role in mentoring you and knows that sometimes skills are best practiced in teams. She will ensure that you have a committed lay mentoring team.[4]
- recognizes the importance of reflecting with you on your experience and engaging in regular dialogue about ministerial practice.[5] She assumes that you value the time she has set aside to meet as colleagues in ministry. She will honor the commitment to a regular time of theological reflection and steward the gift of your reflection time together.
- celebrates the fact that she will learn from you! She affirms that ministry is a commitment to lifelong personal and professional growth. You are bringing fresh eyes to this context along with your own set of experiences and learning from seminary or divinity school.

Third, your supervisor-mentor assumes that God is at work in you. He knows that God, who calls, is more invested in your formation than he could ever be. That's liberating, because it means that your formation for ministry has a horizon that began well before you arrived at your placement and extends well beyond it. The message that Jeremiah received, "Before I formed you in the womb I knew you, and before you were born I consecrated you" (Jer. 1:5), and the good news Paul proclaimed to the Philippians, "God, who began a good work in you, will bring it to completion" (Phil. 1:6), has encouraged prophets, apostles, priests, and pastors to this day. It should encourage you, too!

Given these assumptions, expect the best from your supervisor-mentor. P. M. Forni, cofounder of the Civility Project at Johns Hopkins University, speaks to this directly: "Thinking the best of others is a decent thing to do and a way of keeping a source of healthful innocence in our lives. When we approach others assuming that they are good, honest and sensitive, we often encourage them to be just that."[6] A positive and gracious orientation to your field education placement and to your supervisor-mentor will mean more than can be calculated.

Formation for ministry in this setting is participating in a Spirit-initiated and graced hard work of personal and professional growth. Your supervisor-mentor knows that this also applies to him. When you pray with and for each other you can celebrate what God is doing in this season of learning and growing that is for both of you.

TWO PRIMARY STRATEGIES FOR ENGAGING YOUR SUPERVISOR-MENTOR

Since your supervisor-mentor is assuming your agency in field education, here are two strategies to engage this positive and potent relationship. These involve fair assumptions you can make about your supervisor-mentor.

Enter a Community of Practice

First, she is committed to welcoming and supporting your initiation into a community of practice called clergy or ministerial leader. *Community of practice* is a term coined by Étienne Wenger and colleagues to describe committed learning communities. Wenger defines it this way: "Communities of practice are groups of people who share a concern, a set of problems, or a passion about a topic, and who deepen their knowledge and expertise in this area by interacting on an ongoing basis."[7]

This means that your supervisor-mentor recognizes that you're not just on a journey of acquiring new skills or growing competencies; you're becoming a new person through your formation for ministry. Participation and formation in a community of practice "involves the whole person; . . . it implies becoming a full participant, a member, a kind of person."[8] This is the potential for you in this intentional mentoring relationship that nurtures pastoral and professional identity. Both of you are on the journey! These diagrams show a way of visualizing it.

As members of a community of practice you and your supervisor-mentor are on similar journeys but are in different places on the spiral. In practicing ministry together as colleagues you will find yourselves being drawn further in by the centripetal force of learning and simultaneously find yourselves going deeper in a spiral of deepening competence.[9] Ministerial leaders never stop growing.

You can engage the commitment and goodwill of your supervisor-mentor by risking vulnerability and speaking candidly about your learning goals. The acronym NICE can help:[10]

- **N** is for needs. Don't be afraid to spell out what it is you need to achieve your learning goals. It will be an encouragement to your supervisor-mentor as he works to tailor the learning opportunity to address your goals.
- **I** is for interests. You've come with interests, and your ministerial context will suggest more. Identify what interests you have and share these with your supervisor-mentor. There is room to explore.
- **C** is for concerns. Concerns unnamed are concerns unaddressed. Summon the courage to name what is uncomfortable or concerning so that it can be addressed today. If this feels awkward or you are unsure about speaking directly with your supervisor-mentor, turn to your field education director for clarification and support.
- **E** is for expectations. Expectations can be managed and met by discussing them freely as you create the learning-serving covenant that is part of the field education program. This conversation is important because you and your supervisor-mentor both have expectations. Collegial relationships risk naming them.

This may all sound risky to you. It is. Effective colleagues risk vulnerability with each other. You enter this field education opportunity prepared to take risks.[11] Both you and your supervisor-mentor must summon the courage to admit to imperfection. Each of you is called to practice empathy and respond kindly to each other—and to yourselves. The big payoff for this risk in collegial relationship is discovering more of who you authentically are in ministry. In practice, ministerial teams that take these relational risks foster communities of belonging and release creative energy.

Even with the formation that you bring as an adult learner to this field education placement, it is still a new arena for growth. We can add an "H" to the acronym, for humility. A little goes so far in a learning environment! Listen, observe carefully, and ask your hard questions. You will be exposed to a good deal of the ministerial practice that takes place apart from public worship: administration, care and counseling, time management, prayer, crisis intervention, study, mediation, and relational outreach, to mention a few. Craig Dykstra aptly affirms, "To be a good pastor, you have to be very smart in lots of really interesting ways."[12]

With the addition of humility, NICE can become NICHE: a place that particularly suits your gifts, talents, and personality for nurturing the kind of growth you hope for.

Invite Coaching

You may have experienced coaching in theater, sports, or music. If you had a good coach, you'll recall that he exercised a distinct set of skills to draw the best performance out of you. If he was a great coach, you probably still touch base with him and consider his advice priceless. I'm willing to bet that one of the skills your coach was very effective at is listening.

That's where your supervisor-mentor will begin, simply by listening to you. He will not only listen to your words but do so with the deep discernment of a spiritual director. There is timeless wisdom in James's instructions: "be quick to listen, slow to speak" (James 1:19). What is it that God intends to draw out of you through this collegial relationship and this special time and place for ministry?

Then of course she will ask questions; succinct, powerful, and precise questions.[13] The purpose is to bring clarity and incite initiative. Good questions will be short and open ended: How will you begin? What are your resources? Why is this important to you? What obstacles are standing in your way? Whom might you collaborate with? What is your time frame? This might feel a little threatening, but welcome it. In reality your supervisor-mentor is helping you to pay attention to what is important and gain more perspective on this ministerial opportunity. Since ministry is a fluid and dynamic environment that could feel paralyzing, it also helps you begin. Sometimes the first step in a new and unknown context is the hardest.

Holy listening and powerful questions will be complemented by careful observation. After you have practiced ministry—preached a sermon, visited a hospital room, or led a Bible study—ask for honest and specific feedback from your supervisor-mentor. It would be easy to hear him simply say, "Great job!" Don't settle for that. Affirmation alone misses the point of soliciting feedback. It's much more difficult to improve our performance without constructive feedback. In fact, praise and flattery can be counterproductive when it comes to motivation and actually improving our skills.[14] Contrast "Great Bible study!" with "The skillful way you alternated presenting content and thoughtful questions in the Bible study really helped participants engage with scripture." Specific feedback can reinforce good practice. Or, after you have delivered a sermon your coach counsels, "Don't be afraid to pause and breathe, make eye contact with your people, and then go on. A little space to process the journey you're taking them on can be a gift." Good feedback directs us to future practice. The point is that we can take specific feedback, reflect on it, and reengage that ministerial art to be more effective.

In the chapters that follow you'll recognize that engaging in ministry will always be enriched by honest collegiality, respect for each other's unique gift mix, and mutual mentoring. Engaging your supervisor-mentor well will secure not only greater growth for yourself in a field education placement, but also a colleague in ministry for life.

QUESTIONS FOR REFLECTION

1. What do you assume about yourself as you enter this ministry context?
2. Can you share a story of personal vulnerability in a learning context that resulted in unexpected, even surprising, growth?

SUGGESTED READING

Blodgett, Barbara. *Becoming the Pastor You Hope to Be: Four Practices for Improving Ministry*. Herndon, VA: Alban, 2011.

Johnson, Abigail. *Shaping Spiritual Leaders*. Herndon, VA: Alban, 2007.

Vella, Jane. *Learning to Listen, Learning to Teach: The Power of Dialogue in Educating Adults*. San Francisco: Jossey-Bass, 1994.

Wenger, Etienne, and Jean Lave. *Situated Learning: Legitimate Peripheral Participation*. Cambridge, UK: Cambridge University Press, 1991.

Chapter Three

Engaging with Your Field Education Student

Matthew Floding

You and the people you serve in your ministry context have been granted a sacred trust: the formation of a soon-to-be minister. In partnership with the seminary or divinity school, you function as an off-campus "faculty" member in a laboratory setting with a class size of one or two. Thank-you for taking on this holy responsibility! [1]

Formation is theological in nature, grounded in the character of the Triune God. God is a forming God. When the earth was formless and empty, God formed in a series of actions. God formed by dividing darkness from light and filling it with the sun, moon, and stars (Gen. 1:2ff.). "[T]hen the LORD God formed *adam* from the dust of the ground" (Gen. 2:7). The psalmist in turn celebrates God who formed creation, even the intricacies of our bodies (Ps. 94:9; 139). In Christ, we who are many, God forms into one body (1 Cor. 12:12). We join God in participating in the wonder of persons formed in faith and formed for ministry.

Your significant role in this formation for ministry process also retains an element of mystery. Michael Pollan, in *The Botany of Desire*, provides an apt illustration. [2] Slice an apple in half at its equator and you will find five small chambers arrayed in a perfectly symmetrical starburst—a pentagram. Each chamber holds a seed or two. Imagine that the apple is a Honeycrisp. Should you plant the seeds, each would result in a completely new and different apple—and none of them a Honeycrisp! Each of the students that we as field educators and you as supervisor-mentor are privileged to work with becomes, by the grace of God, the minister that God intends him or her to be, each one uniquely fitted for Kingdom service. This is the mystery and grace of supervision and mentoring in field education—as well as its freedom.

YOU ARE IN A LONG LINE

Seminary and divinity school students in North America have long benefited from the wisdom of experienced ministers. In the North American context, before the first stand-alone seminary came into being (New Brunswick Theological Seminary was established in 1794) and for some generations after in various traditions, pastors mentored young apprentices.

In a small-town New England parish dating back to those days, two pastors whose tenures spanned one hundred years in that one parish continually had students living with them, studying Greek and Hebrew and catching a sense of what ministry was all about before going on to their more formal studies at Harvard. The stipends of these colonial pastor-supervisors were apportioned by the General Court of Massachusetts and included twelve pounds sterling, two barrels of cider, a keg of rum, and ten cords of wood. Now one cannot help but marvel at the commitment of those clergy to serving as teachers, mentors, and tutors in the theological education of those days.[3] (A disclaimer: you may or may not receive such a generous stipend for your service today!)

There is something romantic about the picture of students living in the home of their mentor. On further reflection, you and I know this living/learning arrangement could be disastrous! It does serve to remind us of the extraordinary hospitality required of a supervisor-mentor and the ministry context. In an in-service training for supervisor-mentors, Charlene Jin Lee, professor at Loyola Marymount University, underscored this notion:

> We form people whom we supervise/mentor as students experience us. They learn who we are . . . so we must be authentically present for formation to take place. As we assume the posture of one who is learning and relearning, we provide space where struggles and questions can be voiced.[4]

Hospitality is important but is not the only requisite for a positive learning experience. Lee connects hospitality and authenticity in the learning context and relationship. Supervision and mentoring will require of you humility along with a good deal of intellectual, emotional, and spiritual energy.

There is also a strong coaching element to supervision and mentoring. The following insights (from hockey) could come from any sport or from anyone coaching musicians or actors:[5]

- *Humility*: "Every coach wants to win but not at the expense of skill development." In other words, great supervisor-mentors do an ego check and focus on the joys and satisfactions of seeing growth and development in another.

- *Compassion*: "Great coaches take time to know their players on and off the ice." You can recall your own preparation for ministry experience and all that it demanded of you. In turn, you can invest energy in listening to and showing empathy and support for your student in his or her life situation.
- *Communication*: "Great coaches are able to deliver criticism and praise in a way that players will take to heart." This kind of helpful communication is grounded in your understanding of how this particular student hears and receives feedback.
- *Passion*: "When a coach has a passion for the game and the team, it makes the experience positive for everyone involved." Your love for ministry is contagious. Share it!
- *Leadership*: "Great coaches give their team direction and motivation to help them to reach their goals." You possess an enormous amount of training, experience, and tacit knowledge of what ministry is about. As the leader in the relationship, you can guide and direct your intern into important experiences to ensure the student experiences a breadth of ministry practice upon which to reflect.

Clearly your disposition as supervisor-mentor is extremely significant to this formational experience. This is not to diminish the importance of the student's disposition entering the field education placement. Making this level of commitment to a student's personal and professional development, however, is not easy, for a number of reasons.

First, you may already feel overcommitted. If so, the challenge will be giving your student the kind of attention you would wish you could give to support his or her learning needs.

Second, it's easy to succumb to the temptation to view an intern as free or low-cost labor. Field education is primarily about the student's formation for ministry and only secondarily about the needs of the placement.

Third, doing ministry as a team sport is challenging. The skill of team leadership is something that each of us has had to learn (or we are still learning). We have learned to trust others and to delegate. We also learned that the "body of Christ" is an empowering metaphor for ministry, that each part has value. Each needs to be identified, called into service, affirmed, and celebrated. In that regard, I've claimed Max DePree's metaphor, "leadership jazz," recognizing that we as leaders have a responsibility to empower young "musicians" not only to play according to the requirements of the band and the music, but also to trust them enough to call them out for exhilarating moments of improvisation in the spotlight.[6] Your interns' admiration and appreciation for your efforts will only grow over time as they learn how challenging the work of supervision and mentoring is.[7]

In summer 2015 I asked our students, "What does your mentor *do* that is helpful for your formation?"[8] Their responses are suggestive of the marks of a good supervisor-mentor:

- Honest, constructive feedback.
- Listened as much as he talked.
- She prayed with me every time we met together.
- Genuinely cares about me.
- Wants me to experience all aspects of ministry.
- I was asked what I wanted to learn and taken seriously.
- He was a great sermon coach.
- Has me bring questions/issues each week that I think are important.
- Identified and affirmed my gifts specifically.
- Pushes me to be self-reflective.

Most of what appears on the list is second nature to you, since it is at the core of your pastoral identity. Other items will require effort on your part. Perhaps it's helpful to recall the relationship between Paul and Timothy. Paul joined Lois and Eunice, each participating in God's forming of Timothy's call, and he and Timothy became colleagues for life.

In chapter 1, "Engaging Theological Field Education," I asked students to recall Erik Erikson's developmental theory related to identity resolution. Professionals in student development have long utilized the identity resolution component of Erikson's theory to shape cocurricular programming. Research findings indicate that identity resolution is impacted positively by a learning environment characterized by

- experiences that help the individual clarify her or his interests, skills, and attitudes;
- experiences that aid the individual in making commitments;
- experimenting with varied roles;
- making choices;
- enjoying meaningful achievement;
- freedom from excessive anxiety in the performance environment; and
- taking time for reflection and introspection.[9]

This probably sounds very much like what you try to provide when you host a student. Of course neither you nor your congregation can control the learning outcomes in your student's internship. What you as supervisor-mentor can do is create a hospitable learning environment and open doors of opportunity to practice ministry. To paraphrase educator Donald Schön, "He/she must begin pastoring in order to learn to pastor."[10] In practice, this means that we step back so that our student can step up. This kind of learning-rich environment fosters formation for ministry and vocational clarity.

Formation for ministry is especially challenging at this time in the life of the church. An Alban Institute special report on the impact of the Lilly Foundation's Transition into Ministry Initiative, *Becoming a Pastor: Reflections on the Transition into Ministry*, underscores the challenge: "While the Corinth of Paul's time or the London of Wesley's era experienced their own forms of cosmopolitanism and change, the environments of the early 21st century make the forming of ministers an especially daunting task."[11] The report cites two enormous challenges for those in formation for ministry. First, the explosion of knowledge, pluralism, consumerism, and a host of other complicating factors makes huge demands on what a minister must know to be effective in ministry. Second, with the erosion of thick religious subcultures, there are fewer sources of practical wisdom for the novice minister to draw upon. The Alban report notes, "The communities of practice that their predecessors could count on have disappeared. Increasingly, [new] pastors are on their own."[12]

Fortunately, the study went on to draw a number of heartening conclusions. Among them are three that should encourage you in your work:

- Students value what you have to offer and say so. One participant reports: "I feel like I've learned so much through conversations with [my pastoral mentors] as well as by watching them 'in action.' I appreciate their willingness to share their own ministry experiences or even the thinking behind decisions they've made."[13]
- Seasoned pastors have something important to teach new clergy. Further, when they are given opportunities to teach new pastors, a profoundly valuable kind of practical wisdom becomes available to the church.
- People are formed for ministry not just in classrooms but by practicing the work—and reflecting on it—with others.[14]

These conclusions will certainly not surprise you. Practical theologian John Paver, formerly of the Uniting Church Theological College in Melbourne, Australia, underscores these: "My central belief [is] that theory and practice must critically have a dialogue with and inform each other in order that theological education becomes a unified rather than a fragmented enterprise."[15] In other words, your work with the student, doing and reflecting on ministry practice together, paves the crosswalk between classroom and the world of ministry.

On behalf of all field educators, thank-you for being our colleague.

QUESTIONS FOR REFLECTION

1. Who has had the greatest impact on your ministerial identity? For what are you most grateful?
2. What will bring the greatest joy to you and to your ministerial context as you host this student?

SUGGESTED READING

Floding, Matthew, and Deborah Davis. "The Gift of One Hour: Strategies for Reflective Supervision." *Reflective Practice* 36 (2016): 197–214.

Garido, Ann M. *A Concise Guide to Supervising a Ministry Student*. Notre Dame, IN: Ave Maria Press, 2008.

Lee, Charlene Jin. "The Art of Supervision and Formation." In *Welcome to Theological Field Education!*, edited by Matthew Floding, 17–30. Herndon, VA: Alban, 2011.

Pohly, Kenneth. *Transforming the Rough Places: The Ministry of Supervision*. 2nd ed. Franklin, TN: Providence House Publishers, 2001.

Chapter Four

Engaging Your Context for Ministry

William B. Kincaid

Few experiences compare to the excitement of arriving at and settling into a new place. You are about to discover the uniqueness, promise, and challenge of a community that is new to you.[1] And remarkably, as you engage the life of this new community you may be able to offer a gift to your congregation that only you can give.

If you are like most people in ministry, you exhibit enough interpersonal skills and concern to care well for the individuals in your congregation. If you are like many people in ministry, you demonstrate enough intuition, foresight, and courage to care well for the organizational and systemic life of the congregation.

But have you thought about how well you will care for the place you are about to enter? I am referring to the community or neighborhood where your congregation is located, the place where the congregants and the congregation itself live their lives. Even the most gifted ministry colleagues among us usually do not, or for some reason cannot, care for a place as well as they care for individuals and congregational organizations.

Your congregation has a setting, a context. It didn't just acquire a street name and number once upon a time and begin occupying random space. Your congregation is part of an ecosystem. The ecosystem may be a rural community, a small town, or an urban or suburban area in a larger city.

The congregation you are serving exists alongside various parts of its ecosystem—places of worship, residential areas, schools, businesses, parks, and various community gathering places—and the congregation shares in telling the stories, setting the tone, and naming the priorities that define the community's history, character, and hope. The place where you are serving probably includes a number of wise and creative individuals, as well as its share of quirky people and strange traditions. That will make your life interesting. Sadly, your community likely also features its share of invisible people whose names are not known and whose voices are rarely heard.

As I suggested above, you may be able to offer a holy gift to your congregation. You will notice that I am hedging on this a bit—you *may* be able to offer a gift. A lot depends on how you first encounter and remain present to the depth, detail, and nuance of the community around you. If you see only with the metaphorical blinders that most people wear and capitulate to the default interpretations about your new community, you will have little to offer. You will end up as oblivious, detached, and indifferent as those in and around the church who fail to be present to their own lives and where they live them.

However, if you enter this community with "a properly humbled spirit,"[2] as Kentucky poet Wendell Berry encourages, you will help people see their own community—presumably the community they know best—with fresh cyes. They will awaken to the sacred possibilities of neighborliness and to the holy tending of place.

A properly humbled spirit will allow you to overcome the two challenges that often derail pastors and other ministerial leaders from caring well for a place. The first challenge is imposition; the second is infatuation.

IMPOSITION

When our interpretative frames, familiar landmarks, and faithful companions are missing, our vulnerability can cause us to impose certain things on a context. For example, you may impose on this new community the very best of the place you call home and judge it harshly when the new community doesn't live up to your grief-laden standards, all the while ignoring what was less than ideal about home. Another form of imposition occurs when we need something from a new context that will heal our wounds and ease our disappointments. Or perhaps you expect your new community to grant you the status and respect to make up for the lack of appreciation and standing you believe you have experienced in other communities. In all of these examples you will be asking more of your new community than any place can deliver.

Self-awareness goes a long way in cultivating sensitivity and appreciation for a new place. Like loving anything else, you need to love yourself first. Those who do not or cannot love themselves take out their discontent with themselves on everybody around them, or as in this case, on the place itself. Remember, wherever you go, you take yourself with you.

You cannot be afraid of learning the place as it actually is. Truth about a context sets us free—free to be present to it, free to engage it, free to lead others to live well in a life that encompasses both the congregation and the community.

You will overcome your own imposition by learning, genuinely learning, this new community of which you are now a part. Having your senses on full alert will allow you to recognize and honor what is in your community besides the congregation you are serving. The learning will be further aided by developing an attention span long enough to understand what you are really seeing and hearing.

Your engagement with the context continues as you think theologically about this new place. Sociologists, historians, and anthropologists make incredibly important contributions to our understanding, but where do you perceive God's presence in the community? And in what ways do the opportunities and pain of this context claim the congregation's focus, energy, and gifts?

INVESTIGATIVE SKILLS

Some skills and resources will help you break through the hidden-in-plain-view effect and bracket the often unformed, or at least incomplete, defaults that too many in your new community treat as unquestioned truth. I encourage you to learn your new community by observing, listening, gathering, and interpreting.[3] Here is a brief word about each one:

- Observing—walk through the town or neighborhood and note what you see. Then walk through the area several more times over the period of a few weeks, each time viewing the area from a different perspective (a person of a different race than you, a single parent, an immigrant family, a couple in their eighties).
- Listening—talk with people from the congregation and the broader community who have varying levels of tenure and familiarity with the area about what life is like here.
- Gathering—find historical, cultural, and demographic information about the area from web resources, local libraries, and books written about the area. Save this for the third step; otherwise the data will skew your observing and listening.
- Interpreting—look for what patterns are emerging, what initial interpretations can be trusted, and what information calls for more investigation.

INFATUATION

The second challenge is infatuation. It's good to be excited about serving in a community that is new to you. You cannot engage without some excitement, but there's a difference between eagerly entering a community about which you have a reasonable, informed assessment, on the one hand, and beginning a ministry with an unrealistically optimistic lens.

The signs of infatuation with a community mirror the infatuation we sometimes exhibit toward other people. You may have a case of infatuation (you decide whether it is mild or severe) if you believe your community is so astoundingly perfect that glimpses of paradise can be seen everywhere you look, or if you are convinced that the people have created a conflict-free zone through their amazing love and cooperation toward each other, or if you have finally discovered here exactly the way of life that has so bitterly eluded you everywhere else you have lived. The chances are good that your new community will end up being more of the mix you have found everywhere else. More than likely, you will encounter a great deal of wonder and kindness, but also a fair amount of poorly handled differences and wasted opportunities.

Infatuation burns hot, but we know from interpersonal relationships that it cannot be sustained and does not last. The same is true of your relationship to the community around the church. The letdown hurts as we come to see the community as it really is, but the end of infatuation need not mean the end of the relationship. Instead, you can now be positioned to engage the context over time in a deeper, more realistic relationship. I do not wish pain on you, but frequently a place has to break someone's heart before she can really engage it with her own personal affection and with the hope and love of the gospel. Like everything else in this life, a community responds to understanding and love.

I encourage you to pause and gather yourself so that you can enter into your context for ministry with care and wonder. Recognize the grace that God offers both to you and to this place. Enjoy the hospitality of the place itself. It longs to welcome you. Allow it to do so.

Enter this new place with love, like taking a baby into your arms. Look upon your community as if you will hold it forever. Even if you know you will only serve in this setting for a year or two, attempt to engage this community in ways that would ensure a long-term relationship. Ministry becomes drudgery when we have no fondness for where we serve.

APPRECIATIVE SKILLS

While the move from imposition to learning involves critical investigative skills, the move from infatuation to loving deals in appreciative skills. These skills come alive through the vulnerable sharing of yourself, the active choosing and embracing of this place over and over again. As you move toward your new neighbors with their well-being in mind, your heart will follow. To begin loving your new community, engage your context through the following actions:

- Participate in a community experience, either planned or informal, that takes you outside your comfort zone.
- Identify a prejudice that you carry toward some group or expression in your community and become personally acquainted with someone from that perspective.
- Do something that will quietly benefit the community or some part of it.
- Get on a first-name basis with an invisible person in your community, learn the person's story, and listen for how the person describes his or her life in this community.
- Dream a dream for the community and share it with someone.

Your engagement with this new community involves critical and appreciative skills. I think you can't really love a community until you have learned that community, but in the end learning and loving go together. Your learning and loving will do more than lift up the community through your tender presence, prophetic ministry, and practical wisdom. Your learning and loving also will open the eyes and hearts of those who have been a part of this community for years and maybe even decades. Their learning and loving will result in community uplift as well.

It's hard to imagine a more wonderful gift.

QUESTIONS FOR REFLECTION

1. To which temptation are you most vulnerable, imposition or infatuation?
2. Ask your supervisor-mentor, "What are two or three interpretive keys that you've discovered for understanding this context? How did you discover them?"

SUGGESTED READING

Berry, Wendell. *The Selected Poems of Wendell Berry*. Washington, DC: Counterpoint, 1998.
Norris, Kathleen. *Dakota: A Spiritual Geography*. New York: First Mariner Books, 2001.
Percept. http://www.link2lead.com.
Pew Research Center. http://www.pewresearch.org/.

Chapter Five

Engaging in Ministry Ethically

Barbara J. Blodgett

If I were to give you only one piece of advice about the ethics of being an intern, it would be this: as an intern, you are in the business of giving and receiving trust. Therefore you should prioritize trust over the giving and receiving of anything else. Before accepting something special that you are offered because you are an intern, ask yourself: "Will my receipt of this gift grow or diminish the trust I am trying to build here?"

It's not easy being an intern, in part because of the unique covenantal relationships involved. You may be wondering whether as an intern you are more like a student, an employee, or sort of a consultant or temp. You may be asking yourself whether the rules of academia or the rules of the workplace guide the internship. For starters I would say this: you are engaging in bona fide ministry during your internship, and you have been placed in a position of leadership, but it is also understood that you are learning and will be there only temporarily. And in the end, you only get to be an intern because of the relationship your school's field education program has with your site.

Let me offer, then, an analogy: As an intern, you are sort of like a babysitter who has been given charge of the kids for a day. The analogy is incomplete and imperfect, but it offers at least some guidance.

As an intern, you are entrusted with the care of people who rely on you to know something about how to take care of them. You are entrusted to offer ministry, even while you are at the same time still learning the ropes of ministry. Like a babysitter who may have taken a babysitting course or two (or more) before being called upon to serve, you are not without knowledge and skills. And yet to a certain extent you are learning skills as you go, or else you would have been hired as an employee rather than called as an intern. For this reason, parameters have been set around your practice of

29

ministry. You've been given instructions and guidance about how ministry tends to go in your setting. You've been assured of backup and told how to access help when you need it. You may have been told that there will be spot checks during the course of your internship, in which not only will you be observed and given feedback on how you're ministering, but someone will also make sure the "kids" are doing fine under your care. If your internship was arranged through the school, like a babysitter being hired through a central agency, then you are accountable in two directions: both to the community you are serving and to the school that made your service possible in the first place.

Several kinds of ethical issues can arise given this special relational context. Here I ask and answer a few of the questions you may have and leave it to you to apply my guidance to others that might arise.

What if the "kids" share secrets with me and ask me not to tell their "parent?"

You may initially feel honored if someone at your internship site takes you into his or her confidence. A secret is like a gift, and the sharing of sensitive information may seem like a sign that someone trusts you. It's nice to feel that you have proven yourself to be a trustworthy servant. You may have heard that ministers such as you are supposed to keep confidences no matter what. Moreover, when someone offers you confidential information, that person is often making himself or herself vulnerable and so deserves protection and care. For all these reasons, it may seem counterintuitive of me to advise you *against* keeping confidences, but I will. While your intentions for promising silence might be honorable, doing so is not a good idea in an internship. Your primary moral relationship is to your supervisor, and you should not put yourself in a position of keeping from her information about the members of her own community. If you were to promise to withhold sensitive information from your supervisor, you would be undermining her relationship with those individuals. In addition, your supervisor will be around longer than you will, and it is part of your responsibility to ensure that the individuals temporarily in your care will continue to be well cared for after you leave. These are the arguments against keeping certain confidences, and I might point out that they apply not only to your current internship context but eventually also to situations in which you are one member of a multiple staff team.

What if the "kids" want me to bend or break the rules of the house?

As an intern, you may not always agree with the way your supervisor practices ministry. Supervisors aren't perfect, and beyond imperfection, there are many reasons why they make the choices they do, including theology, polity, and plain old custom. You may have your own valid reasons for doing things differently. You even may have learned at school that your supervisor's procedures don't align with current best practice. But once again, you are there at the invitation of your supervisor and site. Sit down with your supervisor to discuss any practice you're unsure or uncomfortable about before deciding on your own to change it. Don't drive a wedge between the laypeople or clients who have come to trust your judgment and their leaders, whom they must also trust.

For that matter, what if the "parent" wants me to break the rules?

If you are asked to do something as an intern that doesn't feel right, that violates the letter or spirit of your learning agreement, or if you are in some way put in a compromising position because you are the intern, speak to your field education director. Speak up sooner rather than later. Your director cannot help you if she doesn't know what's going on. Moreover, she deserves to be included in any dilemma because she has a stake in the success of your internship and a relationship of her own with the site.

How much should I share back at home about the family I'm serving?

You should share enough information about your internship in your peer group to facilitate your becoming a better and more trustworthy intern at your site. Let learning be the gauge. The whole group learns from your experience. Talk about the curses and blessings of your internship so that you and others may grow in your knowledge and skill as ministers. When it comes to sensitive site-specific information, the generally accepted rule of thumb about peer group conversation is that what's said in your peer group stays in your peer group. Don't take this advice to mean, however, that you are free to share incidental and irrelevant information about site members, especially if that information is private. Don't gossip about your site or complain fruitlessly about it. Don't use stories from your internship as entertainment.

What if I grow to like some of the "kids" in the family better than the others?

It's natural to be drawn toward certain individuals more than others. But like all ministers, interns serve everybody. The covenantal relationship you entered into with the site was meant to be broad and inclusive. If you were to select some people to become close to, you would inevitably exclude others. An inner circle necessarily implies an outer one, and if the former feel privileged by having been singled out as the intern's friends, the latter feel marginalized. The same reasoning applies, by the way, to forming romantic relationships at your internship. Romantic relationships additionally carry the danger of exploiting the power differential between you as an intern and the person you are supposed to be serving. I'll say more about that in a minute.

Should I have contact with the family on social media?

Social media has become an effective tool for ministry. Correspondingly, let effective ministry be your gauge. Join and contribute to social media sites that the whole community uses to build up the whole community, but limit your use as an intern only to those. Maintain a boundary on social media between your personal life and your life as an intern. Even then, remember that many forms of social media have built into their design the tendency to blur boundaries that can otherwise be more easily observed. Nothing you put on social media is totally private. Everything you put on social media creates a trail of some kind. Develop wise practices now.

So who's got the power?

Like a babysitter, you have a good deal of power over the exercise of your service, but so do the parents. If "babysitting" has gone well in the past in this family, the laypeople or clients at your site will likely look up to you. Indeed, some of them may not distinguish you from the full-time permanent ministerial leaders and grant you the same status and respect. This means that you must be careful not to abuse or exploit the power you have. You must be a trusting and trustworthy leader at your internship site. But as an intern you are also a follower. Your power is circumscribed by your role. This means that you must be equally careful not to let yourself be abused or exploited. Sadly, faith communities are not immune to sexual harassment and other forms of misconduct. The US Department of Education defines sexual harassment as "any conduct that is sexual in nature; is unwelcome; and denies or limits your ability to participate in or benefit from a school's education program," so you are protected from such conduct by Title IX insofar as your internship is an educational program.[1] Insofar as you are an employee, you are also protected by the US Equal Employment Opportunity Commission, which recognizes that behavior does not have to be overtly sexual in nature to count as harassment; the creation of a hostile work environment is also harassment.[2]

Once again I would remind you that your field education director is your ally, advocate, and protector throughout your internship experience. If something isn't right, or doesn't feel right, discuss it with your director. Field education directors cannot address what interns choose not to disclose and would much rather learn of adverse situations sooner rather than later.

Should I accept gifts?

My advice would be to think twice before accepting gifts of significant value during your internship. The reasoning here is that gifts represent, or appear to represent, a quid pro quo—something given for something received. In most cases no expectation is attached to the giving of a gift, but you should err on the side of preventing even the appearance of being influenced by one. While local cultures vary greatly on the practice of gift giving, so that you should consult your supervisor, in general I recommend that you receive only gifts given collectively by your entire community and at the end of your internship rather than at the beginning.

How you handle yourself during your internship will be valuable practice for the rest of your ministry. Thanks for listening, and good luck!

SUGGESTED READING

Blodgett, Barbara J. *Lives Entrusted: An Ethic of Trust for Ministry*. Minneapolis, MN: Fortress Press, 2008.
Blodgett, Barbara J. "Ministerial Ethics." In *Welcome to Theological Field Education!*, edited by Matthew Floding, 115–132. Lanham, MD: Rowman & Littlefield, 2011.
Bush, Joseph E., Jr. *Gentle Shepherding: Pastoral Ethics and Leadership*. Atlanta, GA: Chalice Press, 2006.
Gula, Richard M. *Ethics in Pastoral Ministry*. Mahwah, NJ: Paulist Press, 1996.

Chapter Six

Engaging in Theological Reflection

Matthew Floding

Want to get better at something? Do reflection. That's how a basketball player improves her three-point shot and an actor improves delivering his lines. They take the shot or speak the lines, reflect on technique and how they mentally and physically executed the performance, and go back and practice. This works even better with a mentor.

Ministry requires it all: all that you are and all that you've learned. You become a new kind of person. It takes everything to minister with authenticity, integrity, and faithfulness. By authenticity I mean putting away the façade, any false self in order to minister as God made and gifted you, with a deep sense of self-awareness and humility. Integrity is about theory and practice connecting coherently within you. It means you are becoming, by God's grace, a more integrated person and that your story and your practice of ministry have integrity with the capital "T" tradition, church catholic. At the same time, you're aware that you minister within a small "t" tradition. Yours could be the freshest expression of church at the local microbrewery or a historic church with a plaque on the pulpit that says, "Received from Holland, 1656, Cost Complete with Hour Glass, 25 Beaver Skins."[1] Whatever your tradition, you want to minister faithfully within it. I named "humility" because as my tradition has it, we're "reformed and always reforming."

Theological reflection is a huge component of this. The point of theological reflection is that it actually helps you discover more of who you are; how precious and meaning-full the Tradition is; and the joy of ministering to, with, and receiving from the Christians you journey with. For example, I can't say at the Table, "Grant that being joined together in Jesus, may *we* . . ." or at a graveside, "In *our* sure and certain hope of the resurrection to eternal life through Jesus Christ . . ." without the feeling of being swept up, with my people, in the great river of God's life in Christ by the Spirit.

THEOLOGICAL REFLECTION WITHIN FIELD EDUCATION

Yes, there is a technical definition, and it merits exploration. Within a field education placement, theological reflection is *"reflection upon lived, embodied experience in ministry that seeks to make sense of practice and form reflectors in habits for competent ministry."*[2]

In your field education placement you'll have experiences that both unsettle and enliven you. Rule of thumb: where there's energy, press the pause button and reflect. Your body and your mind are calling you to pay attention. These kinds of experiences in ministry deserve as close a read as any textbook. Most of your shared reflection time will be with your supervisor-mentor and with peers. Working pastors know the richness of reflecting with a colleague or a regular peer reflection group on ministry experiences.[3]

Vulnerability is critical. You don't have to look good in the story. It's like the sign on our church's playground: "Play at your own risk." Take the risk!

Making sense of your experience in order to foster authentic ministry with integrity that is faithful—if not perfect—will involve a process that looks something like a Venn diagram. This gets at the Trinitarian complexity of ministry. Your experience (one circle: naming what happened, how others may have experienced the event, sorting out your feelings and capturing images that come to mind) enters into a deep conversation with the Tradition (second circle: scripture, theology, history, and liturgy) with an attentiveness to God who is at work throughout and bigger than the situation (rectangle). However large the overlap, there will be untidy areas outside the integrative center. That's real ministry.

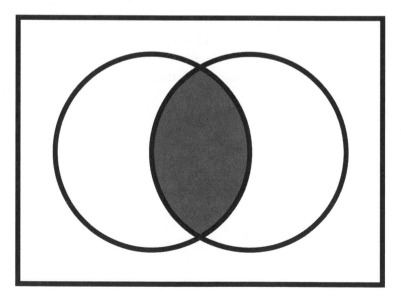

There are many theological reflection methods. In field education you'll be introduced to some of these. Your supervisor-mentor expects to engage in reflective supervision with you.[4] You can try out different methods of theological reflection appropriate to the event that prompts it.[5] Most approaches expand on basic inductive method: What?, So what?, Now what?[6] That may feel a bit clinical. My counsel is to invite the Spirit's counsel and correction and begin by accurately describing what happened in its context. Your reflection partner(s) will be invaluable for drawing out pertinent information that escaped you. Explore the question, "Why did this happen?" Imagine how others involved may have felt and experienced the event. One word of caution: human beings and congregations are not formulaic, but deep mysteries that make all of our wonderings tentative.

Other kinds of questions get at the intersection of the Venn diagram from the other circle. How does scripture speak to this kind of event? Where might it be situated in the grand narrative of scripture? What biblical images come to mind? What theological themes intersect with this experience? What is at stake theologically? If you reflect with clergy from other traditions, alternative, interesting, and helpful questions will surface.

WHAT DOES IT LOOK LIKE?

What does it look like? Great question! I think we can discern formation resulting from reflection at work in characters in the Bible. I'm writing just after Pentecost Sunday, so this example comes to mind. Jesus promised the coming Comforter and told the disciples to wait in Jerusalem. They were gathering daily for their upper room prayers and reflections with the women leaders, including Mary, the mother of Jesus. When the wind of the Spirit blew into Jerusalem and into their lives, someone from the crowd asked, *"What does this mean?"* Peter, who undoubtedly reflected on his amazing reclamation, reconciliation, and restoration by the resurrected Jesus, claimed his commission to feed and tend Christ's sheep.

Peter interprets their shared experience by connecting it to a scriptural text from the prophet Joel. In the last days it will be, God declares, that "I will pour out my Spirit upon all flesh, and your sons and daughters shall prophesy" (Joel 2:28). He even connects it skillfully with covenant promises made to David and Israel. Ultimately, Peter's sermon prompts the crowd to ask another theological question, *"What should we do?"* (Acts 2:37). Peter doesn't miss a beat, but calls upon the crowd to respond to the new covenant by repenting and being baptized in the name of Jesus the Christ. He assures them that they will receive the promise of forgiveness of sins and the gift of the Holy Spirit.[7]

Okay, granted, you're not a biblical character, but the same Spirit is at work in you. Formation for ministry is still the result.

Kathryn lives in Friendship House.[8] It's a residential ministerial formation opportunity in which three seminarians and a person with an intellectual disability practice intentional Christian community with other similarly arranged apartments.

Kathryn was completely disarmed by the unconditional love she experienced from her roommate, Jill. When Kathryn moved in she assumed she would be "ministering to" Jill. It turned out to be not the opposite, but as she describes it, "something far better, a mutuality that gave life."

Kathryn began searching for pastoral positions during her senior year. She discerned one in particular that might be a good fit. She applied. She was given an opportunity to interview with the search committee over the phone. They liked what they heard and invited her for an in-person interview. Kathryn asked Jill to accompany her to the interview. She informed the search committee that her apartment-mate would be accompanying her. It surprised the search committee, but they too were disarmed by Jill, and she became part of the interview process! Kathryn later confided that this was part of her discernment process. "Living with Jill and doing our reflection time together as an apartment has so deepened my understanding of the Kingdom of God that I want to serve where removing barriers to full participation in church will not be an issue." Kathryn was extended a call; she said "yes" to God's vision for the church and world and "yes" to that congregation.

Practice theological reflection consistently, and over time it will form you in faith and form you for ministry.

YOU'RE NOT THE ULTIMATE GOAL

But here's the thing. You're not the ultimate goal of theological reflection. Your participation in the ministry of Jesus for the sake of your congregation (or nonprofit community) and for the world so loved by God is. In other words, your reflective practice will be used by God to fashion a reflective people who themselves are being transformed. Evidence of this is a mark of sustained and patient pastoral engagement and the transforming work of the Spirit.

I was speaking with a pastor friend who shared a story of this kind of reflective transformation. This pastor had patiently led the congregation to discern that frequent Communion was encouraged by Jesus, grounded in the early church's practice seen in scripture and faithful to their own theological tradition.

Weekly Communion became the practice of the congregation. Any change takes time to get used to, but for the most part this new practice was well received by the congregation. Not by everyone, of course. The pastor heard about this, too.

The steady rhythm of Eucharistic hospitality, patient liturgical catechesis by the pastor, and the unexpected gifts that came with frequent Communion stirred up something. One day the pastor received a letter from a person who had been less than enthusiastic about the change.

It seems that the change of practice had unsettled the person's church routine. To his credit, and no doubt the Spirit's, the man engaged more deeply with his weekly experience, scripture, and his own theological convictions. He reflected on his personal transformation: [9]

> First, almost every Sunday, sitting where I do, as people go to the Table, I can look forward, or across, and see men and women I know; people who are suffering, carrying burdens, visible or invisible; and I can silently pray for them, as I know some of them do for me.

Jesus took a loaf of bread, and after blessing it he broke it, gave it to the disciples, and said, "Take, eat; this is my body."

> Other mornings, I am desperate, hoping there will be some magic in the cup, willing to crawl on my knees to the Table . . . to say, "I believe; Lord help Thou mine unbelief. . . ."
>
> Or to be reminded, we are one in the Lord, those folks I revere and those I secretly shake my head at "from a great height"; all belong to Christ, not to me. His blood covers them just as effectively as it does me. . . . Each week the world erases that from the blackboard of my heart; at the Table Christ patiently writes it back.

Then he took a cup, and after giving thanks he gave it to them saying, "Drink from it, all of you; for this is the blood of the covenant, which is poured out for many for the forgiveness of sins."

> And I am old. I now read the obituaries every day, and too often, there is a colleague; my latest sun is sinking fast, my race is nearly run; I cringe at what lies ahead, I fear the darkness. But, each and every Sunday, I hear, stretching all the way back to my childhood, the voice of the pastor, the words of the Word: For as often as you eat this bread, and drink this cup, you do proclaim the Lord's death, until He cometh. It matters.

For as often as you eat this bread and drink this cup, you proclaim the Lord's death until he comes.

The author closed with an apology: "Sorry. Not well put into words."

Your commitment to theological reflection matters; not just for your sake, but for theirs.

QUESTIONS FOR REFLECTION

1. Can you recall and describe an experience in which your reflection brought about personal change?
2. What biblical stories and theological themes are woven into the core of your identity?

SUGGESTED READING

Blodgett, Barbara, and Matthew Floding, eds. *Brimming with God: Reflecting Theologically on Cases in Ministry*. Eugene, OR: Pickwick Publications, 2015.

Click, Emily. "Ministerial Reflection." In *Welcome to Theological Field Education!*, edited by Matthew Floding, 31–43. Herndon, VA: Alban, 2011.

Killen, Patricia O'Connell, and John de Beer. *The Art of Theological Reflection*. New York: Crossroad Publishing, 1999.

Kinast, Robert. *Let Ministry Teach: The Art of Theological Reflection*. Collegeville, MN: Liturgical Press, 1996.

Chapter Seven

Engaging in Sustaining Spiritual Practices

Deborah K. Davis

After seventeen years as a hospital chaplain I experienced a powerful sense of compassion fatigue. My ministry was caring for those who were suffering; responding to crises; and being present for patients, doctors, nurses, and the staff. I was well placed as the person who brought calm into stressful situations; acceptance in the face of judgment; honest hope when confronted with wishful thinking; and a safe place for people to confess their problems, failures, hopes, and dreams. I was the mother of three energetic sons, a wife, the moderator of the presbytery, and an on-call chaplain twenty-four hours/ seven days a week. I was doing everything I loved, and I was totally, absolutely, burnt out. I was empty. There was no living water left in my well.

To address my compassion fatigue I enrolled in a weeklong seminar in spiritual direction. I imagined I would spend this week multitasking: getting some time away from the pressures of my life, receiving training that would enhance my work as a chaplain, and beginning a book I was contemplating on chaplaincy. So much more happened!

As I slowed down to pray, meditate upon scripture, sit in silence, and receive spiritual nourishment, the Holy Spirit began to revive me. I drank deeply from the well of a variety of spiritual practices that invited me to a closer relationship with God. During my quiet times my thoughts, which usually focused on problem solving and list making, were replaced by a new ability to listen for the voice of God guiding me. I was given my life back by being introduced to the concept of developing spiritual practices in my life that would reconnect me to God, the true source of living water.

41

BRINGING SPIRITUAL ORDER TO ONE'S LIFE

During that week a small book by Thomas Kelly, *A Testament of Devotion*, came into my life. This slim volume by a Quaker writer helped me to begin to sort out my life. Kelly says that answering the many calls within us in a life-sustaining manner means coming to understand our "emphatic responsibilities."[1] He describes emphatic responsibilities this way: "A loving God does not burden us equally with all things, but considerately puts upon each one of us just a few central tasks as emphatic responsibilities. For each of us these special undertakings are our share in the joyous burdens of love."[2]

I discovered that life becomes simplified when dominated by faithfulness to the concerns that have truly been chosen for me. I uncovered my individual emphatic responsibilities by attending to the guidance of God during my prayer, study, and work time. For me these were being a mother, wife, and chaplain, the three most important parts of my call. Everything else needed to move to background responsibilities. That meant letting go of many of the committees I was on, a board I chaired, and writing projects I was always imagining and never getting to. This simplification was a challenge and a relief.

Once I named my emphatic responsibilities, the challenge was to discern what spiritual disciplines I would engage in on a regular basis to sustain my life, my relationship with God, and the relationships with those around me. I did this by establishing a rule for my life based on the Rule of St. Benedict. A rule is based on commitment to living in a balanced way within yourself, with others, and with God. As Brian Taylor states in *Spirituality for Everyday Living*, "To live under a rule means to enter consciously into a process of growth in grace by undertaking specific spiritual disciplines."[3] You are not developing a rule for your life so that you can "become disciplined, as if that is the primary virtue."[4] The rule is undertaken as a means of freedom in God.[5] A balance of prayer (spirit), study (mind), and work and play (body) is essential so that you do not concentrate in one area to the exclusion of the others.

The key to experiencing the rule as sustaining is that it is invitational: something that you are drawn toward. As you begin to practice your rule it is important to recognize human frailty. You need to be able to laugh at yourself and move on when you waver in following your own rule, rather than be driven by a perfectionism that causes you to give up once you falter.[6] This is my rule: I take a daily prayer walk. I meet with other ministers weekly. I meet monthly with a spiritual director. I take a silent retreat each year. During these times of study, prayer, and work I listen for God's word to me to guide me in my life. This is a simple rule, and for me it has been life changing!

I believe that ordering your life through spiritual disciplines has a better chance of enhancing your life as a person and a pastor than any other self-help program out there. As you are reading this you may be thinking that you are too busy for daily prayer, too scheduled to meet on a regular basis with other ministers, too consumed by ministry to spend an hour a month with a spiritual director, and have too many family responsibilities to spend a week on retreat. You may be thinking, this is a good idea, but you will do this when you have more time (e.g., finish this school year, finish your internship, graduate from seminary, accept your first call, raise your children, write that next book). You may be overwhelmed by the myriad responsibilities that you have as a student, seminary intern, wage earner, and family member while serving as a field education intern. You may be reflecting on the spiritual disciplines that you tried in the past and thinking that they were tedious, boring, and unimaginative. You may say that you lack energy and time for a spiritual life.

The truth is you never will have more time than you do now . . . ever. Psalm 118 says, "This is the day that the Lord has made." This is the only day you have. Today is the day to rejoice and to make a plan for embracing your spiritual life. Please, for your sake, identify those spiritual resources in your life that you find invitational and that connect you to God. Then make a rule for yourself so you can do these life-giving practices faithfully. Here are some suggestions.

ENGAGE IN LIFE-GIVING PRACTICES

Prayer: Different types of prayer include prayers of petition, intercession, lament, confession, praise, thanksgiving, and blessing.[7] These prayers can be offered as breath prayers, silent prayers, or spoken prayer. Praying can be done in the morning, noon, or evening; throughout the night; and when you are washing the dishes, planting flowers, mowing the lawn, or doing other daily activities. Praying also goes well with all kinds of exercising: walking, running, swimming, doing yoga, shooting baskets, jumping rope, sky-diving! Meditation is another form of prayer that can be life changing. Choose the method(s), time, and manner of prayer that will bring light to your day and allow you to connect with God, both speaking and listening.

Scripture: Immersing yourself in scripture becomes a joyous and transforming part of life when you find the way to engage it that gives you new insight into who God is. For some people that can be through reading a chapter of the Bible every day. For others it means using the *lectio divina* method of meditating upon scripture.[8] Some people find translating from the original language (Greek or Hebrew) a way to slow down and hear familiar words anew. Others find that memorizing a verse each week and meditating upon that verse throughout the week gives new life. Memorization of scripture so that it is written on the soul provides for some a rich and deep method of taking scripture into their very being. The most important thing is to discover a way to hear scripture as God's word to you and embrace that method!

Writing: Writing in a variety of forms can help you reconnect with God as you let go of the spinning in your head to put down your thoughts in a creative or linear way. For some people journaling each day (or week or month) the events of their lives helps them gain a new perspective on where God is in their lives. Others have found that writing a spiritual autobiography is a great way to discover the theological themes that have been guiding their lives.[9] For some people writing case studies, reflections, or verbatims and reflecting on these with others helps to reframe, revise, and renew their method of handling and thinking about different issues in their lives. Some enjoy reflecting on their lives, and the way they are confronting theological and spiritual issues, through blogging or simply writing poetry. Is there a form of writing that will invite you to know God more deeply and to live your life more fully?

Spiritual friendships: There are acquaintances, friends, and spiritual friends. Spiritual friends are those people with whom you can take off the mask, reveal who you are, become vulnerable, and talk about where God is acting in your life. Who are your spiritual friends? Can you set up a regular time to meet? Will you trust your soul to be held tenderly by another and offer the same kind of reciprocal care on a committed, regular basis?

Meet with a spiritual director: Some people find one of their spiritual friends to be a spiritual director or mentor. They usually meet with a spiritual director on a regular basis (biweekly, monthly, quarterly) to reflect on their lives in relationship to the spiritual, theologically, and sometimes (un)Godly things with which they are struggling. This relationship is less reciprocal and focused on you getting the time you need—devoted to you and God—on a regular basis. Part of my call is to sit quietly with people as a spiritual director, on a monthly basis, and to listen for what I hear God saying to them through me. This is not therapy or life coaching. Is it time that you found someone with whom you can sit in a holy space and listen for what God has to say to you and how you will respond to life's inevitable challenges?[10]

Worship: Worship is a way to connect with God every day and in every way. You can worship by yourself and with others, in the holy congregation, in the field, on the mountain, around the dinner table; in the morning, at noon, and in the middle of a sleepless night. Where are you finding time to experience God in a way that has its foundation in gratitude?[11]

Exercise: Your body is as important as your mind and spirit. St. Benedict included specifically in his rule the need for all the monks to work as well as pray and study. I would add that using your body to play is as important as using your body to work! What is your body saying to you about how you have been treating it? What kind of physical activity can you joyously embrace? Maybe you can combine it on a regular basis with your prayer life! The point is to bring your whole, healthy self to ministry, and to thrive in your life.

Creativity: Allow God's inspiration to move through you as you paint, draw, sculpt, play music, listen to music, dance to music, dance by yourself in a field of dreams, write poetry, or photograph a sunset or a baby's face. All are ways to be in touch with the Holy Spirit's life-giving force! Your creativity is a spiritual resource that can bring renewal to your soul. What part of your creative self have you been longing to explore but have not allowed yourself to because of time, pressures, responsibilities, or some other reason? Is there a creative aspect of yourself that is beckoning you to come forward and give it space and life? [12]

I invite you to develop an amazing, invitational rule for your life in order to begin to engage your spiritual practices in a way that leads to renewal, rest, restoration, and new life—throughout your lifetime. These are just a few of my thoughts! What are yours?

QUESTIONS FOR REFLECTION

1. What are your emphatic responsibilities? Who is God calling you to be? What is God calling you to do? What are the responsibilities in your life that it is time to let go of?
2. What are the spiritual disciplines that you would love to include in a creative rule that would be an invitational addition to your life?
3. What are structures (timing, place, frequency) that you need to put in place so that this will be a sustainable, life-giving rule?

SUGGESTED READING

Brother Lawrence. *Practice of the Presence of God.* New York: Doubleday, 1977.
Cameron, Julia. *The Artist's Way.* New York: Jeremy P. Tarcher/Putnam, 2002.
Guenther, Margaret. *Holy Listening.* Cambridge, MA: Crowley Publications, 1992.
Hunsinger, Deborah. *Pray Without Ceasing: Revitalizing Pastoral Care.* Grand Rapids, MI: Eerdmans, 2006).
Kelly, Thomas. *A Testament of Devotion.* New York: Walker, 1987.
Taylor, Brian. *Spirituality for Everyday Living.* Collegeville, MN: Liturgical Press, 1989.
Wakefield, Dan. *The Story of Your Life: Writing a Spiritual Autobiography.* Boston: Beacon Press, 1990.

Chapter Eight

Engaging in Personal Self-Care

James Marshall

Where I did my graduate training in clinical psychology, they held high a slogan that I'll paraphrase: "If you're planning to do therapy on others, then you'd better be willing to get therapized yourself first!" Fair enough. Yet strangely daunting. It was week ten of a mandatory ten-week group psychotherapy process—a session dedicated to final thoughts and wrap-up. At the start of this final session, one of my fellow students, as if a spokesperson for the rest of the indoctrinated crew, protested: *"Dr. Benner, how is it that every one of us has spilled our guts but somehow through this whole group experience Marshall hasn't? We had to take the risk but he didn't!"* Our sage doctor had been waiting for this. He had read my required autobiography. *He* knew. He knew the narrative I had never voiced to others or to myself; of repeatedly reaching for, yet losing hold of my father, whom I deeply loved and desperately needed but could not save, who was killing himself with alcohol.

As nine faces watched, Dr. Benner turned slowly toward me. His kind eyes were disarming and compelling. He asked one potent question: *"Jim, when you were nine years old . . . and you were taking care of your father: who was taking care of YOU?"* A frightening, profound sadness and grief flooded me. During the next thirty minutes, as tissues mounted into a pile at my feet, I heard my lips speak words assembling, declaring my story for the first time. This had become a sacred place.

By necessity, in childhood I'd learned that I must take care of myself emotionally, that reliance upon others for psychological support was only a setup for disappointment. However unconscious its evolution, this assumption solidified into an internalized core belief: *I can and must take care of myself, without depending on other people.* The belief we form about how we should manage our distress is what I call our *emotional creed*. Mine had strategic value for me. It fostered a strong self-sufficiency and spared me the disappointment of repeatedly asking for help that would not come. It was not healthy for a child, nor is it healthy for an adult, especially a pastor. The more we embrace an unhealthy emotional creed that isolates us from the support and care we need from others, the greater the risk of existential loneliness, depression, self-medicating, and failures in personal and professional life.

For me, a healthy emotional creed sounds like this: *It is right and good, though often scary as H---, to admit my distress, to judiciously seek support, to accept the love and help of others. I will learn and practice this self-care to the best of my ability each day.*

What is your emotional creed? What message will you write on your heart that will enable others who are safe to gain access to it, to abide with you, for your sake and that of all those who love you? Let me suggest that you write and endeavor to live out your own version of this creed through three essential self-care practices: journaling, peer support, and pursuit of clinical psychotherapy.

SELF-CARE JOURNALING

Self-care journaling is a writing practice that creates a space and platform for you to gain and maintain essential personal emotional insight and self-awareness. While there is no single best way to practice this discipline, let me offer two approaches that can become naturally integrated into your life.

The first approach is responsive journaling. This involves writing out your perceptions of any event that you have experienced as very emotionally significant in work or personal life, positive or negative. Capturing experiences for which you are grateful boosts personal resilience and can help you maintain a sense of balance in your life outlook amid the hardships of ministry. Describe what happened, who was involved, what made it so special, and any meaningful images you want to remember. Sharing these experiences selectively with family, friends, and parishioners can also lend them hope and encouragement while deepening your shared relationships. In your field education placement you can use your supervisor-mentor as a trusted conversation partner.

Responsive journaling is also a potent process to help manage and process highly distressing circumstances. It can help you shift from feeling overwhelmed and helpless to gaining a sense of empowerment even when you can't control the outcome of events. And this can help prevent depression and serious complications in relationships. If, for example, a congregant has made an alarming public accusation about you, rather than ignoring your internal signs of distress or launching into reactive behavior, welcome them as cues to do something smart for you. That is, just notice and document upsetting thoughts, painful emotions, and related physical sensations. (Imagine now what those might be in this situation.) Then take time to reflect carefully on the question: "Is my thinking about the situation accurate?" Finally, ask: "What is the wisest, healthiest way to handle this experience?" You may conclude: "That was hurtful. But I think I may be reacting too defensively. . . . Do nothing yet, but wait, reflect, and pray." Or the answer may be: "Yep, my thinking is accurate and I may need to assert myself. But I still need to pray first and seek some good input or counsel from others."

Another journaling approach that is highly valuable in self-care is regular wellness journaling. This involves scheduling a set time (preferably weekly) to respond in writing to a revised version of a classic compassionate question: "How is it with my soul?," or if you prefer, ask: "How am I doing, really?" The goal of this regularly scheduled inquiry is to prevent the impacts of accumulated distress that can occur when we feel too busy and absorbed over an extended period to reflect in real time after tough situations. In your writing, address your spiritual vitality, overall mood, outlook on personal relationships and church life, and sense of physical well-being. Your answers may lead you to important insights and plans to address issues or make changes in physical self-care, or lead you to one of our next two self-care practices. For me, self-care journaling has often included gut-level pouring out to the Lord, listening for His voice, being the recipient of invaluable guidance, and a deeper sense of intimacy with Him.

PEER SUPPORT

While you can certainly enjoy a measure of informal support from those within your church, it is preferable to seek the deepest lay support from those beyond your congregation. That's where peer support comes in. This is a special relationship that provides essential support, affirmation, and human caring that can replenish and protect a pastor's personal sense of well-being. It prevents the existential aloneness and emotional isolation that places spiritual leaders at risk. Peer support is especially crucial for pastors because finding people with whom you can feel safe to entrust your vulnerable stories is not easy. Boundaries with parishioners get blurry, and divulging private information can get risky since you share dual relationships: they are friends in one sense, yet are those you serve in an official capacity.

Look for peer support from an individual who is ordained or has a real understanding of church ministry, who is spiritually and emotionally mature; is stable in his or her well-being and relationships; evidences strength in holding confidences; and displays a deep regard for the power of listening free of the compulsion to fix, rescue, or offer unwanted advice. Once you identify a good candidate, agree that meeting together for this purpose is an experiment to which neither of you is initially committed, since it may take a few meetings to discern if in fact you are a fit for each other. Agree also that the sharing you do together is not a substitute for any needed professional counseling, nor does it preempt the kind of personal sharing essential in your relationships with your spouse (if married) or your supervisor-mentor. Many formats for peer support can work, and it can be mutual. Most important, set a format that works for both of you and keep it simple. Initially, after feeling assured that your peer supporter knows enough about you and your background, explore your personal wellness goals. Then at your regular meetings you can enjoy catching up, sharing your status related to your goals, gaining support, and seeking the Lord's help through shared prayer. Be sure to meet in a space that provides an appropriate level of privacy.

PURSUIT OF CLINICAL PSYCHOTHERAPY

Your willingness to seek help from a licensed mental health professional both preventively and when personal mental health or relationships are threatened is an essential part of living out a healthy emotional creed. For the most complex psychological and relationship issues, and when you need assurance of the highest level of confidentiality, there is no substitute for professional mental health assessment, diagnosis, and treatment. In selecting a therapist, you will want to consider three criteria to assure fit:

• The person's attitude: willingness to cooperate and answer your questions, humility, degree of caring, and so forth.
• Ability and competence to be effective in helping you.
• Your sense of "fit" with the person as a human being, clinically and spiritually. That is, how comfortable you would be working with him or her.

It's preferable to prioritize those who are highly recommended by someone you know well if you are seeking treatment for similar issues. But such personal referrals are not always possible. Consider also using online search engines designed to find therapists by specialty and location. When you do find one or more clinicians you're interested in, make a brief phone call to assess them on the three criteria. After offering a brief description of your counseling needs (what you want to achieve or overcome), consider asking the following questions, which any qualified therapist should respect and be happy to answer:

1. What is your training and experience in helping people with needs like mine?
2. Is this an area of particular specialty for you?
3. What evidence-based treatment (EBT) will you use to help me with this?
4. What experience do you have working with clergy, and how do you integrate faith into your treatment approach?
5. What are your credentials (education, licensure, affiliations with professional organizations)?
6. What are your fees, and does insurance cover your services?

Initially, a qualified therapist will work to build an alliance with you so that you feel safe. He or she will carefully assess your needs, seeking refined descriptions of your struggles and strengths, and rule out immediate risks to your stability. Then the therapist will work collaboratively with you toward a clearly defined treatment plan you can easily understand and believe fits your needs. The therapist will also provide a written confidentiality agreement for you to sign that articulates how your private information will be protected and specific conditions under which it may be shared. The duration of therapy varies greatly depending on the nature and severity of your concerns and issues. Clinicians should be able to provide an approximate estimate of the time it will take to achieve your goals, which might include relief of emotional pain or other symptoms, new skills to manage distress or succeed in relationships, or new insights empowering you to make important life decisions. Usually sessions last about an hour and are scheduled weekly, unless intensive needs call for more frequent treatment. Visits are less frequent if feasible to achieve the desired outcomes and as you maintain progress. Treatment generally ends when the client is confident that his or her goals have been reached.

Embracing the self-care proposed in these three practices is the farthest thing from narcissism. It represents the means to maintain firm ownership of personal responsibility for well-being and is strongly implied by Jesus in his second commandment to "love your neighbor as yourself."[1] Your choice to practice intentional self-care is also a preventive for what Episcopal priest Barbara Taylor Brown described as *"her soul slipping away"*: *"Drawn to care for hurt things, I had ended up with compassion fatigue. Drawn to a life of servanthood, I had ended up a service provider. Drawn to marry the Divine Presence, I had ended up estranged."*[2]

It also models a way of life for your church family that can foster and safeguard their vitality. This is my prayer for you.

QUESTIONS FOR REFLECTION

1. Define your healthy emotional creed and wonder with compassion toward yourself what internal blocks you might need to overcome to fully embrace it.
2. How would you like to shape and practice each of the three elements of self-care? Who will you share this work with?

SUGGESTED READING

Burns, Bob, Tasha Chapman, and Donald Guthrie. *Resilient Ministry: What Pastors Told Us about Surviving and Thriving*. Downers Grove, IL: InterVarsity, 2013.

Hamman, Jaco. "Self-Care and Community." In *Welcome to Theological Field Education!*, edited by Matthew Floding, 101–113. Herndon, VA: Alban, 2011.

Marler, Penny Long. *So Much Better: How Thousands of Pastors Help Each Other Thrive; The Sustaining Pastor Excellence (SPE) Peer Learning Project*. St. Louis, MO: Chalice, 2013.

Shapiro, Francine. *Getting Past Your Past: Take Control of Your Life with Self-Help Techniques from EMDR Therapy*. Emmaus, PA: Rodale Books, 2013.

Chapter Nine

Engaging in Preaching

Jason Byassee

I owe my ordination to field education. I went to seminary to study God, not to serve God's people. But my seminary made us go and do these internships in these little godforsaken places. I went because I had to. And I was surprised to learn that I loved it. I'd talk about God, and the people would respond with encouragement. I'd visit in people's homes and feel the presence of God so strongly, they should put up a plaque. I saw ministry up close and with all my senses, and I was hooked. I went from an aspiring scholar to a pastor in the church. One of those summer internship churches bought me an alb. It's still the only robe I ever wear.

So if you're reading this book, you're off to serve a church as an intern, and I'm jealous. God is going to do something remarkable in you and in this church during y'all's time together. A student more senior than I was gave this simple piece of advice to us newbies at an orientation talk: "Love the people and preach the gospel." It's a good summary for all of ministry.

LOVE THE PEOPLE

"Love the people": it's harder than it looks! Often we go into ministry because we see it being done so poorly and we intend to do it better. That can make us arrogant about the church as it stands now. They can smell that on you. Some of these people are hard to love, too. Some are so dysfunctional the church is the only place they're ever invited to. So they're there every time the doors are open. They're there not because they're good at people skills, constructive debate, or effusively offering praise. They're there because they're not. Further, you're young. At least you're young in the profession of ministry, maybe also young in years. If you're not passionate now, something's wrong. And that passion for things to be better can sound like an implicit criticism: "You're doing it wrong."

Some friends of mine in ministry have shown magnificent impatience. They had some major agenda—like they wanted to make the entire church more biblical, evangelical, and revivalist overnight. Or they wanted the church to be entirely and full-throatedly gay-affirming yesterday. Or they want divestment from Israel. Or they want us all to adore the blessed sacrament. Or whatever. And they preached some sermons, wrote some articles, protested a little, and bailed for some "better" church (hint: there isn't one!). Matt Miofsky, pastor of The Gathering United Methodist Church in St. Louis, advises us this way: "Don't expect them to start where you're finishing." That is, you feel strongly about whatever because you've thought about it, read about it, sweated and prayed over it, had passionate conversation, and worked it out. As you preach or teach you're proposing this thing you care deeply about to people for whom it's much more new. They're not prepared. They don't have it all worked out, prayed through, sweated over. And often in our magnificent impatience we expect them to come along immediately. No one can do this. Someone with actual data wrote that we can only question 5 percent of what we believe at any given moment. First sermons from interns can sound like they want all listeners to question 100 percent immediately. Won't happen. Affirm your shared 95 percent hard, and they may go with you for the 5 percent you really want to nudge them on. The short time of our internships can exacerbate our impatience. We feel we have to lay all we got on 'em before our ten weeks or semester or year is up.

Here's the thing about ministry: it's Jesus's ministry before it's ever ours. And Jesus is God's infinite patience with the world. God could, presumably, get the world God wants from us forcibly, immediately. And God does not. God waits. And presents his Son to us, crucified and risen. And woos us by his Spirit. A God who has chosen to save in so foolish a way as cross and resurrection presumably has no interest in efficiency. The Triune God may indeed have fired your devotion to your pet issue(s). God will get the world God wants eventually. In the meantime we get to join in: point others toward it, help imagine together the kingdom that's coming. We don't get any points for being right and lecturing those who are wrong; far from it. We need to preach the way God rules: patiently, slowly, nudging rather than crowbarring, asking for an ounce of the patience God is.

PREACH THE GOSPEL

"And preach the gospel." This one should be first, of course. But if we don't love first, we don't get a hearing. The gospel is the good news of God's repair of the world in Christ. And the gospel on Sundays is always strained through the shard of one particular biblical text. How does this text function as a prism showing us the beauty of the whole thing? I imagine, being new, you're ready to throw your whole self into this first sermon. I was so geeked to preach my first time that I blurred through my whole sermon in seven minutes. Folks thanked me—they got to lunch early! I still remember whole points I made in that sermon, and I can't remember the title of the last sermon I preached on a Sunday. Throw yourself in—we can risk a little excessive enthusiasm. But recognize what you're doing is a small thing. You're asking them to take one step toward heaven this morning—not all the steps. Preaching is like eating: it's a cumulative discipline. Sermon hearers sometimes complain they can't remember what their minister preaches. Fine, I say, you can't remember what you had for lunch last Tuesday, can you? But if it's healthy, over time, you'll be healthy. If it's not, well. As you prepare, imagine you're fixing them a meal. You'll do your best. They'll know their role is to praise you, the new cook. But your job isn't to serve them their last meal ever (we hope!). Nor is it to wow them with your range and depth of ability. Your job is to cook as well as you can, to honor them who honor you with their presence, and then to take part in the banquet yourself, where Christ is both host and food. And more than anything, your job is to praise God. If you love God in the pulpit, they'll love God more.

The gospel is the good news *of Jesus*. If a certain Jew from Nazareth didn't have to rise from the dead for the sermon to work, then start over. It is good news normed by the biblical text. This doesn't mean you should do an information dump of all the historical criticism and linguistic work you've done on the text. That's for seminaries. In church they're interested in the text insofar as it teaches about God. So sure, tell us about verb forms, text criticism, whatever. But tell us about God eventually. The gospel is local and particular: God gets born in one place, grows up in another, serves in several, and dies in another. And God is passionately interested in the details of the place you're at. So learn the place. Ask about its history, its characters, its mythology. And integrate them into your preaching. I recently learned that a geographical shorthand for a remote place here in western Canada is Carrot River, BC. What a perfect analogy for the wilderness. In seminary I became convinced that violence was unfaithful. But I sat and listened to World War II veterans talk about the most morally significant moments in their lives. And they weren't moments of actually doing violence. They were ancillary things. One man taught an illiterate fellow soldier how to read. Another told of a colleague who was left behind enemy lines by his unit, escaped, and then wounded himself to go home: "I'm not fighting for people who didn't fight for me." Had I gone in with judgment I wouldn't have heard any of these stories. One man told me of a fellow soldier who tripped in Italy, broke his ankle, went to a hospital ship, and sank with it and all on board that night. He shrugged with wonder. What "right" did he have to still be here? None.

That's a place of grace. Is it any accident he was the most joyful man in our church?

ENJOY THE FREEDOM

As an intern you have an ambiguous sort of authority. You're not really clergy yet. You're certainly not a member of the church. You're a guest. The church will be proud it's helping train a future minister to bless a future congregation. They'll be obliging about mistakes—they know you'll make 'em. So you have a certain safety net beneath you. Take risks. So many ministers, churches, and people just play things safe. Don't. Practice risk taking in your internship. Remember the fragile egos of us senior ministers. We're as needy and bruised as anyone else, maybe more. One supervisor I had exploded in tears one Sunday. I didn't know what to do, until her husband pointed to the door and slammed it behind me. I knew to pray for her and to learn from her how to hurt and heal on the job. I remember another supervisor who was mildly defensive after my first sermon was well received. "If I had time I could do some of that stuff you did in your sermon," he said, referring to a refrain I used (not exactly a time-consuming thing to plan). But you can also do your supervisor a solid. You can say stuff he or she can't. If the senior gets heat for it, he or she will beg off: "Ah, it's just the intern." And you can create things your senior can't. One legend at Duke, my alma mater, is of a summer intern at a big church in Indianapolis who led a summer course on just war and pacifism. Hundreds of people came. They'd never heard this stuff before. For all my praise of patience above, never underestimate what God can do through you. God made the universe with dirt and salvation with a grave. What can God do with you and them as y'all become a "we" together?

EMBRACE THE FEEDBACK

I remember well some of the best pieces of supervision I got on my preaching. One mentor sent a two-page, handwritten letter praising most of what I'd done and then telling stories on himself to illustrate indirectly what needed to be better. He illustrated Pope John XXIII's advice: "Overlook much. Correct a little." Another mentor came to hear me unannounced. I thrilled to see his face out there. Then I watched it go blank, contort, and check out while I was talking. When I wrote and asked for feedback he said, simply, "Preaching is very hard." He couldn't be more right. Many preachers go years without seeking feedback on their preaching even from their own congregation. Use this internship time to start doing just that. It'll teach you how to be open to receiving genuine affirmation and constructive feedback. I assume you have a real gift or two for preaching, or you wouldn't be here. And I assume you have an area or two that needs real work in your preaching, or else God would already be through with you. Work like mad making the strength better. Do a little work to make sure the weaknesses don't sink you.

Mostly learn to love it. Preaching is beautiful. It participates in the Word by which God made the universe; it participates in the Word of God that the Spirit inspires called the Bible. I miss preaching to the same people weekly. When I preach now it's as a guest, which feels awkwardly like a one-night stand (That was great! See you again never!). To "love the people and preach the gospel" you have to know them, to know what hurts, what thrills, what God is doing through this unique congregation in which you're bound up for a short time. This internship is like an engagement. You'll be married soon enough. And it'll be over in ten minutes. So too will all your ministry, even if you stay at it for decades. Life is unbearably brief. You may as well do something worthwhile with it. Like preach. Wrestle with God's angel over scripture and emerge with a limp. Talk about the risen Christ on the road on the way to breaking him and pouring him out for others. And rejoice.

Most people don't get paid to do something they adore.

QUESTIONS FOR REFLECTION

1. When have you had the opportunity to speak about God? What was that like for you?
2. Invite your supervisor-mentor to describe his or her journey as a preacher. How has God developed and continued to grow his or her preaching voice?

SUGGESTED READING

Augustine. *On Christian Teaching*. Translated by R. P. H. Green. New York: Oxford University Press, 2008.

Bolz-Weber, Nadia. *Pastrix*. Nashville, TN: Jericho, 2013.

Byassee, Jason, James Howell, and Craig Kocher, eds. *Mentoring for Ministry*. Eugene, OR: Cascade, 2017.

Long, Thomas G. *The Witness of Preaching*. 2nd ed. Philadelphia: Westminster, 2005.

Peterson, Eugene. *The Pastor*. San Francisco: HarperOne, 2012.

Chapter Ten

Engaging the Liturgical Arts

Josie Hoover

Imagine this: you walk into a church one Sunday morning expecting to hear a good sermon, listen to inspiring music, and connect with your church family members. You're fairly new to the congregation and have enjoyed both the traditional and contemporary hymns that are normally sung each week. Between the opening prayer and the acknowledgment of visitors, a group of women process into the sanctuary in prayerful and serene postures adorned in flowing yet simple garments. Quietly moving to what appears to be their starting points, the women lower their heads and place their hands at their sides. Suddenly a familiar song pours through the sound system, and the women begin to move to the music. Once you see them dancing in unison with meaningful expressions on their faces, you become mesmerized. The next thing you know, you begin to cry uncontrollably. Dance has never impacted you in this way before, so what makes this moment so unique? Is it that you experienced God in a new and unique way? Is it that you witnessed dancing in the *church*? Did God speak to you in a way that inspired you to do a little more than what you were already doing?

That's what I experienced when I first saw liturgical dance in the church. The dancers moved with ease, confidence, and purpose; at that moment, I knew I wanted to dance for God! Think about the first time you were exposed to the liturgical arts, no matter the location. How did it make you feel? Did you want to jump up from your seat to join the actors, singers, poets, and dancers at any given moment?

When you think about the liturgical arts, you're most likely thinking of acting, singing, dancing, visual arts, or the spoken word. You might believe that these artistic forms are activities normally seen at special programs or seasons of the year, like Christmas, Easter, Youth Sunday, and Mother's Day. Since you want to explore the liturgical arts in this field education placement, I want to encourage you to think about the liturgical arts as a transformative form of worship. When you actively engage in it for the benefit of the congregation, think of it as a part of your personal worship extending directly into corporate worship with others. In fact, your art is prompting others to worship. If you thoroughly enjoy the arts and cannot see them outside of your life, maybe *this* is a central theme in your calling! [1]

The liturgical arts change you. They are powerfully transformative because they tap into something deep in one's personhood. Your spiritual life may grow in new ways. For example, your prayer time may become more intentional, more focused and disciplined. Your art form has theological implications! Now is the time to explore this aspect of your call, in a field education placement where you can practice the art and do theological reflection on it.

But I am getting ahead of myself. Let's explore the transformative and purposeful nature of the liturgical arts through six affirmations that emerged from my doctor of ministry studies. [2] My liturgical art is dance. That will be reflected in the affirmations. Which art form do you want to explore? Allow yourself to make the translation to speak to your liturgical art(s).

THE LITURGICAL ARTS EMPOWER YOU TO RESPOND TO YOUR CALL

The story of Samuel (1 Sam. 3:4–11) is about hearing God's call and responding faithfully. In this placement engage the liturgical arts with an "ear for hearing" God's call. The concept of investigating my call through dance was introduced by my former dance ministry director. Rev. Faye Richie-Chandler, artistic director and founder of RUACH Worshipping Arts Ministry and executive pastor at Without Walls Christian Church International, believes the liturgical arts provide a way to help one discover their destiny for life. Through her shepherding, many artists have devoted their lives to serving Christ.

When you engage the arts, you are engaging in your call to ministry. The arts speak because they engage us as whole persons. As you engage your art, ask yourself if you approach it with dedication, commitment, and tenacity. As you practice your art, are you just going through the motions, or do you realize that your ministry has implications? Are you performing, or are you in ministry? When you are in your element and you see it as a calling, you understand at that moment, it is no longer about self-gratification but instead, it is about edifying others. [3]

THE LITURGICAL ARTS ARE PURPOSEFUL

Ecclesiastes 3:1–8 reminds us that "there is a season." The liturgical arts are very versatile but need to be purposefully employed. Dance can serve different purposes at different times. Depending on the occasion, one might offer a dance of healing, deliverance, celebration, victory, praise, or worship, among others. Your gift of dance is not simply inserting a dance at any point in a worship service; rather, it should be prayerfully placed within the worship service and not serve as a filler. Neither should any other liturgical art. Invite your supervisor-mentor to discuss the path to discerning the roles of the Holy Spirit, faith, scripture, and discipline in the art you feel called to explore. You *and* your medium have a unique purpose, and you should be attentive to it at all times.

THE LITURGICAL ARTS EMBRACE DISCIPLINE

Hebrews 12:5–11 reminds us that discipline is important as a liturgical artist and a disciple. Discipline can deepen your relationships with God and with others. I've found that it can also diminish egos, as dance (and other liturgical arts, for that matter) can bring out the best and worst in people. Spiritual practices such as praying, fasting, service, and submission will help you develop discipline, and they in turn will discipline you as you embody the ministry of dance.[4] To engage the liturgical arts through discipline and spiritual practices is instrumental to experiencing transformation.

THE LITURGICAL ARTS ARE SPIRITUAL GIFTS

Yes, dance is an expression of spiritual gifts. Lists like 1 Corinthians 12:4–11 ground spiritual gifts in the Giver of gifts. Your opportunity is to deepen your understanding and experience how your spiritual gifts and talents are utilized through the ministry of liturgical dance (or other arts). For example, a dancer might be gifted with her hands to create pageantry aids like flags, banners, and streamers to accompany movement. Someone else may be naturally gifted in hospitality and able to help plan events on behalf of the group. As you engage in your liturgical art in this field education placement, what other gifts can you contribute to the body of Christ?

THE LITURGICAL ARTS AFFIRM YOU AMID BROKENNESS

Psalm 147:1–11 engages brokenness and healing as gifts from our great and compassionate God. Invite conversation with your supervisor-mentor (or trusted counselor) about insecurities and distractions from your past that might pose a hindrance to fully dancing in a way that is purposeful, effective, and transformative. This is critical because dance and the liturgical arts in general are an embodiment of the whole person with extreme vulnerability. Masking and channeling fears can be easy. The difficult part is to address those fears and internal brokenness. You may experience personal healing and self-acceptance through this time of vulnerability as you look within yourself. Embracing yourself in healthy ways will shape how you interact with others and with God.

THE LITURGICAL ARTS INVITE THE ANOINTING OF THE HOLY SPIRIT

Anointing was critical to the ministry of Jesus (Isa. 61:1–2; Luke 4:18). The same is true of us. Personal assessment is important. Reflecting with your supervisor-mentor and with laypersons on your journey as a liturgical artist will shed more light. Ask yourself: "Am I called to the ministry of ____ (name your art form)?"[5] "How did God show up when I exercised my art?" "Was my artistic effort available to the Holy Spirit to inhabit and bless God's people?"

My experience, along with the dancers I studied, is that in making these affirmations while practicing liturgical dance, I and others did experience personal transformation, receive clarity about our call and purpose for life, and feel equipped for the demands and discipline of ministry. As the dancers engaged the liturgical art of dance, they understood it to be a ministry of restoration, deliverance, healing, love, and peace.

As you engage and explore the liturgical arts in this placement, I am hopeful that you will experience joy. You will also be answering your call to ministry. You will lead people to their own spiritual transformation, as mine began when tears fell when I first encountered liturgical dance in church. Your artistic interactions will give them permission to explore the liturgical arts as well. Finally, your artistry can instill a sense of hope and peace in a world that seemingly becomes more tumultuous each passing day. As you engage in the liturgical arts, know that you are a vessel loving God and sharing God's love toward humankind, which are the great commandments.

QUESTIONS FOR REFLECTION

1. What expressions of the liturgical arts has this congregation or ministry already experienced?
2. What concepts or topics will be helpful for you to discuss with your supervisor-mentor to engage the liturgical arts meaningfully in this context?

3. Which of the six affirmations are you most interested in exploring?

SUGGESTED READING

Adams, Doug, and Diane Apostolos-Cappadona. *Dance as Religious Studies*. Eugene, OR: Wipf and Stock, 2001.

Begbie, Jeremy, ed. *Beholding the Glory: Incarnation through the Arts*. Grand Rapids, MI: Baker Academic, 2001.

Butler, Stephanie. *My Body Is the Temple: Encounters and Revelations of Sacred Dance and Artistry*. Fairfax, VA: Xulon Press, 2002.

Foster, Richard J. *Celebration of Discipline: The Path to Spiritual Growth*. New York: Harper-Collins, 1998.

Chapter Eleven

Engaging in Pastoral Care

Willard Walden Christopher Ashley, Sr.

Engaging in good pastoral care involves a lifetime of learning, listening, leading, and loving. Good pastoral care is life giving. Good pastoral care restores, refreshes, and renews. Bad pastoral care causes harm. Individuals and families are hurt. Congregations are damaged. Ministries are derailed. Faith is challenged.

Here are some of the lessons I've learned personally and professionally during my thirty-four years as a senior pastor, twenty-four years as a theological educator, and twenty years as a marriage and family therapist/psychoanalyst.

PERSONAL

The phone rings. "My husband suffered a heart attack. Please come to the hospital." Downstairs at home is your child, dressed and ready to go out for a fun day with you. What do you do? The first group of lessons is about balance. Learning to balance the multitudinous pastoral care responsibilities with your life is challenging. Learn this valuable lesson early in your career. Now, in this field education placement, would be a great place to start.

Ego

I put ego first because it is the one that we don't like to admit AND it impacts the other lessons. If our ego is in check, challenges are more easily handled. If it is not, challenges are more difficult, and the impact of our care is diminished. Second, if our ego leads us to low self-esteem, we can quickly become toxic and create long-lasting damage to individuals, families, congregations, and communities.

Pastoral care requires a healthy ego. We have a proper confidence in our competence. However, we are NOT wedded to a narcissistic desire to fulfill our ego needs at the expense of others. Pastoral care is not about you! We engage in pastoral care to provide quality care to others.

Family

If you have a family, make sure your family feels it is your priority. Learn how your supervisor-mentor balances his or her family with the role of caregiver. Pay attention to the stories and narratives from pastors' kids and spouses (both your own and others). Learn to distinguish among family, close friends, and parishioners or patients. Invest in quality time with your family. Learn to protect that time. *You are irreplaceable to your family.* Vacations, short trips, fun activities, educational events, meals together, memorable moments, and shared spirituality help keep our families healthy and intact. In short, do not let your family feel neglected. Listen, learn, and love!

Healthy Boundaries

Discuss with your supervisor how to set healthy boundaries. Discover when and how to be comfortable saying "No." Learn to identify times when you are not available or the task is beyond your skill set. Be honest with yourself. Guard against the notion that you are irreplaceable. Be careful not to be so important in your ministry (in your own mind) that your family and close friends take a far backseat and resentment builds. Schedule date night, family fun days, and outings with friends and learn a hobby. Do not be available 24/7!

Self-Care

Make time for good self-care. Some aspects of ministry are draining. Some are energizing. Routinize times for rest, relaxation, and rejuvenation. Try keeping a journal to track the impact caring for others has on you. Take note of the people or situations that give you positive energy and know the ones that drain you. Look for patterns.

Other important things to consider:

- Make regular visits to your health-care provider. Be sure to take advantage of annual checkups. Listen to your body.
- Monitor your nutritional habits.
- Exercise; give yourself permission to build this into the rhythm of your week.

- Make regular visits to your therapist. Look for a therapist who offers a sliding scale if insurance is an issue. There are also federally funded health centers and mental health facilities.
- Take time to play.
- Employ healthy sexual habits.
- Learn to manage your stress.
- Embrace your creativity.

As a student it's not too soon to monitor and manage your finances wisely. Budgeting now to live within your means will help it become a disciplined practice once you start receiving regular compensation. Define your financial priorities. Seek counsel from practitioners. Your particular faith tradition may have guidelines on finances and stewardship. Learn the difference between wealth and income.

PROFESSIONAL

Preparation

You are in seminary to receive an academic theological education for ministry. Commit to being a lifelong learner. Start now in this field education placement. Work with your supervisor-mentor to identify additional journals, books, and materials that address your specific areas of ministry interests. Some ministries or pastoral vocations require certification or licensure. If this is part of your call, identify the requirements and necessary training.

Now would be a good time to explore theories encountered in your pastoral care courses to see how they work in pastoral practice. Take, for example, family systems theory. A good grasp of family systems theory can help pastors avoid being trapped awkwardly. Congregations, organizations, and institutions are emotional systems. Ask your supervisor-mentor how she or he understands this dynamic within the congregation.

The other part of preparation for pastoral care is learning about yourself. One seasoned, downtown, tall steeple pastor told a group of Princeton seminarians that to engage in ministry one needs (1) a voice coach, (2) a mentor, and (3) a good therapist. AMEN! Essential to pastoral care are regular visits to your therapist. Find a good one and go, regularly!

It takes courage to face our own issues, transferences, countertransferences, projections, family history, attachment patterns, and power dynamics. Clinical pastoral education (CPE), workshops, clergy counselors, mentors, and therapists can help us identify our strengths, blind spots, and growing edges.

Priorities

Learn now how to set priorities. Let your supervisor-mentor be of help in testing out your approach as a gentle accountability partner.

Who is in most need of a pastoral visit today? How much time do you need to prepare for Bible study or the sermon? How much time is necessary to provide proper pastoral care to a family that has lost a loved one or lost its home because of a disaster? Must you attend the board meeting this week or watch your child compete on the high school team? Use this field education placement to learn the discipline of setting priorities.

Opportunities in Pastoral Care

Pastoral care consists of more than hospital visits and counseling, even though both are key to good care. Let me expand the options and suggest eight opportunities for engaging in pastoral care.

Advocacy

Advocacy is an essential part of pastoral care. Clergy and lay leaders in pastoral care are advocates. We write reference letters for persons seeking employment and letters to judges for those caught in the legal system. We work with social service and governmental agencies along with institutions to ensure our seniors receive all the benefits their years now afford them. We attend community planning board meetings and collaborate with other clergy or lay leaders to bring about positive change to our communities. Clergy and lay leaders advocate for better schools, safe neighborhoods, fresh food in our supermarkets, fair trade products, just sentencing for convicts, and quality services regardless of the zip code. We read, digest, distribute, and critique the twenty-year plan in our local community. Advocate for those not at the table.

Counseling

Take full advantage of all the opportunities to learn about pastoral counseling. Research shows that persons often go to clergy first for counseling. We can serve as triage to identify needs and make appropriate referrals. Couples go to clergy for premarital counseling and sometimes as the precursor to a divorce. Pastoral counseling includes offering individuals, couples, and families spiritual models for handling conflict, loss, and challenges.

This is difficult work, and usually what we are privileged to hear is only the tip of the iceberg. There is always more. Remember we are triage, not the counselors. We actively listen. We will not and cannot learn it all in one visit (nor should we try).

Allow me to offer specific guidance about caregiving in your role as a field education student:

- Know your limits; you are not trained as a counselor. If you have degrees or training in counseling, this is not your role at your field education site.
- Remember to always engage in "active listening." Check in during the conversation and repeat the words of the person to ensure that you heard and received accurately what he or she said. "I heard you say . . . Did I capture your words, thoughts, and feelings accurately?"
- Practice being fully emotionally present with the person. Mirror or play back the emotional affect of the person you are counseling. Acknowledge his or her feelings. Work to be comfortable with expressions of rage, anger, or deep sadness. Do not personalize them.
- Allow persons to share a wide range of emotions, from joy to rage.

Here's a hospital case scenario: Rick is a member of the congregation. Rick learned that he needs surgery in two days. The surgery will require that Rick miss a month from his job as a construction worker. He was admitted to the hospital. The senior pastor asked you to visit. Picture the scene. Rick is anxious, angry, and concerned about how this surgery will impact his life, work, and ability to continue doing the things he loves to do. Your first task is to be fully emotionally present to give Rick permission to express his thoughts and feelings. Second, gently encourage Rick to discuss his fears and concerns with you. Be a safe person, which means Rick can be honest and blunt and emote, without you running away or being judgmental. Third, help Rick talk about his faith and other spiritual resources that can be of help as he faces this surgery and its aftermath.

Education

Teaching is part of pastoral care's expansive reach. How does this field education placement engage these care opportunities?

- Teaching parents best practices in parenting.
- Helping families learn how to weather storms of conflict.
- Teaching couples how to be a couple.
- Enabling congregants and neighbors to learn about retirement, assisted living, living wills, and estate planning.
- Resourcing congregants and neighbors to learn about budgeting.
- Giving guidance to persons who seek to monitor what their children watch on television.

When you are in leadership in congregational ministry, invite subject experts to address the congregation on topics of interest. Read and be able to suggest helpful books on some topics your congregants face. You can't be an expert in everything; defer to those more skilled and be secure in your calling.

Health Care

Clergy are expected to be present during times of hospitalization, sickness, and long-term illness. Pastoral care often is simply being able to manage anxiety (both others' and your own). Expect high stress in times of health crisis and loss. Clergy and congregations can express care proactively, too.

- Host health fairs.
- Encourage early screening for common diseases. Set a good example by being screened.
- Know medical specialists in your community. Develop a resource list to help persons in need of a medical procedure to have a professional explain what to expect before, during, and after the procedure.

Relationships

Build relationships. Make it a priority to know the community. Meet elected officials. Introduce yourself to law enforcement, firefighters, store owners, educators, local employers, and service providers. Meet and befriend the local clergy and caregivers. Collaborate on projects and objectives that you have in common. Following the attacks in New York City on September 11, 2001, my own commitment to being networked relationally proved to be invaluable.

Social Justice

Good pastoral care requires a commitment to stand for and with persons who are marginalized, disenfranchised, and invisible to society. We are responsible for the care of souls. Social justice is a call to be inclusive in our ministry and challenge others to do the same. Dr. Martin Luther King Jr. demonstrated that pastoral care demands courage to stand on one's convictions and strategic confrontations to bring light to darkness. Pastoral care asks clergy to be interrupters of policies, media, stories, rhetoric, politics, and the world as it is. We give voice to matters of racism, sexism, sexual orientation, and practices that diminish one's humanity. Ours is a quest to help people receive holistic care in all the various aspects of their lives.

Spirituality

Prayer, sacred literature, and religious practices are primary tools that pastoral caregivers utilize to help facilitate healing. In our doing for others, we must not neglect our need for our own spirituality. Read carefully chapter 7, on sustaining spiritual practices.

Visitation

Major in visitation! Learn how to make excellent pastoral care visits, be they to the hospital, home, or workplace. Ask your supervisor-mentor to take you along on pastoral visits. Learn by observing and participating, then invite being assigned to go on your own visits. You will be surprised by what you learn during a home visit. More important, you will rejoice at the healing and hope a simple home visit can generate. Visitation shows interest. It demonstrates that you care and the person matters. Know that the fastest way to alienate and cause damage is *not* to visit people in their time of need. On the other hand, you can be a tremendous source of healing with a well-placed pastoral visit or phone call (you may find it impossible to visit in person).

FINAL THOUGHTS

Good pastoral care involves a lifetime of learning, listening, leading, and loving. It is work that requires personal and professional reality checks. It is also work that is filled with opportunities to make a difference in the lives of many people. Besides learning and avoiding common traps and pitfalls, may this field education placement provide experiences of caregiving that are truly rewarding.

QUESTIONS FOR REFLECTION

1. What thinkers, books, and mentors left the biggest impression on your supervisor-mentor in regard to pastoral care? What insights did they give to your supervisor-mentor?
2. What are your top three strengths and challenges in offering excellent pastoral care? What is your plan to develop your identified strengths and work on your challenges?
3. Where are the federally funded health and mental health facilities in your community? Who and where are counselors your congregants or you can engage on a sliding scale?

SUGGESTED READING

Brown, Sandra. *Counseling Victims of Violence: A Handbook for Helping Professionals.* Alameda, CA: Hunter House, 2007.

Dykstra, Robert, ed. *Images of Pastoral Care: Classic Readings.* St. Louis, MO: Chalice Press, 2005.

Jun, Heesoon. *Social Justice, Multicultural Counseling and Practice: Beyond a Conventional Approach.* Thousand Oaks, CA: Sage Publications, 2010.

Kujawa, Sheryl A., and Karen B. Montagno, eds. *Injustice and the Care of Souls: Taking Oppression Seriously in Pastoral Care.* Minneapolis, MN: Fortress Press, 2009.

Chapter Twelve

Engaging in Evangelism

John G. Stackhouse, Jr.

I'm not an evangelist. Likely neither are you. But we are both called to evangelize, and pastors are expected also to train people in evangelism. So how can we do what we're not gifted to do, let alone train other people in it?

When I say I'm not an evangelist, I mean that I do not evidence what the New Testament calls the spiritual gift of evangelism. Spiritual gifts, as you know, are abilities bestowed on Christians by the Holy Spirit to contribute to the building up of the Body of Christ. People with the gift of evangelism are especially effective in "midwifing" conversions: in presenting the good news of salvation in Jesus so clearly and cogently that people tend to believe it and begin a new life of discipleship. And I don't have that gift.

I'm reasonably good at presenting the gospel to people. I do it in my theology classes, my books, my journalism, and media interviews. And some people, at least, think I do it cogently.

But people don't tend to make decisions for Christ when they hear me speak. In fact, I've never had anyone phone in to a radio show, or write a letter to an editor, or come up to me after a lecture and say, "Hallelujah! I've just become a Christian." People with the gift of evangelism, however, have this kind of thing happen to them all the time. If I weren't so holy, I'd resent them for it.

Still, I am glad to do what I do. And what I do, and what you do, and what every Christian is to do, is contribute to the Very Big Task Jesus issued us in the Great Commission: not merely to provoke people to "conversion experiences," but to *make disciples* of Jesus (Matt. 28:18–20). We each and all are to contribute our gifts toward helping men and women, boys and girls, come to faith in Jesus and then grow up in full maturity (Col. 1:28).

Pastors, then, might have the gift of evangelism. Those called to plant churches likely do, in fact. But most pastors don't. Instead, they have what

73

every Christian has: the obligation to be ready to give an answer for the hope we have within us (1 Pet. 3:15), the ability and the willingness to both commend and defend the gospel. When the occasion arises to introduce someone to Jesus, to initiate someone into the Christian Way, then we want to be able to do that properly, right? And that's what this chapter is about.

Yes, I know that proselytizing has a bad name nowadays. I know that apologetics is a dirty word in academic religious studies, smacking as it does of condescension and bellicosity.[1] Can't we just live our lives, let other people live theirs, and if someone for some reason happens to want to join our group, then we can provide them with the welcome materials?

Alas, no. For pastors do not trade in merchandise or fashion, but in the Word of Life. Evangelism is literally a life-and-death matter: how to enjoy the abundant life promised by Jesus (John 10:10) and how to prepare properly for death. We dare not be reticent about the Best News Ever. As outspoken entertainer and atheist Penn Jillette (of the magic team Penn and Teller) puts it bluntly:

> I've always said that I don't respect people who *don't* proselytize. I don't respect that at all.
>
> If you believe that there's a heaven and a hell, and people could be going to hell or not getting eternal life, and you think that it's not really worth telling them this because it would make it socially awkward—and atheists who think people shouldn't proselytize and who say just leave me alone and keep your religion to yourself—
>
> How much do you have to hate somebody to *not* proselytize? How much do you have to hate somebody to believe everlasting life is possible and *not* tell them that?[2]

So let's proceed! Pastors evangelize mainly through three modes: pastoral conversation, preaching (especially on "high days" or other special occasions), and equipping others to evangelize. To do these things well, pastors need to develop three areas of competence.

First, pastors need to know the gospel. They need to have in mind a concise, coherent, and comprehensive account of the fundamental Christian message. The gospel is the answer to the question, "What is wrong with the world, and how is God saving it?" So what do you need to say as an adequate summary of this good news?

I don't mean to imply that one has to drop a canned message on everyone on every occasion. It is striking that Jesus himself seems never to outline an entire "gospel presentation" anywhere in the . . . Gospels. But obviously if we are going to selectively deploy elements of the gospel as befitting this or that occasion in conversation or preaching, we had better have a firm grasp of it.

And we had better know where each element comes from in Scripture. We all know that proof-texting is not an adequate way to do theology. But we need to be able to crack open a Bible and say, "See? I'm not just making this up." Then the encounter shifts from you and your interlocutor to *the Bible* and your interlocutor, and that's better, right?

So whether you arrange the gospel materials narratively (e.g., creation, fall, redemption, consummation) or analytically (e.g., What's the nature of reality? What's the highest good we can hope for? What keeps us from that? What can be done to realize that highest good?), you need to know them well, and from Scripture.

Second, pastors need to know what obstacles typically impede their audience's access to, and embrace of, the gospel. One cannot prepare for every question and every complaint. But experienced pastors know that the majority of questions in a particular society boil down to a handful of perennial concerns. In our place and time, those tend to be questions about religious pluralism, sex and sexuality, science/rationality, imperialism and violence, and especially the problem of evil. So we should prepare ourselves to give decent answers to these questions—not to allay every fear and nicely resolve every mystery, but to demonstrate at least that Christians are aware of these problems and can offer reasonable responses to them.

Moreover, we need to know what obstacles stand in the way of our *particular* audience. This requires listening, asking follow-up questions, and listening some more. As a professional question-answerer myself, I have found that the first question someone asks, or the first objection someone raises, usually is not in fact the most important reservation he or she has about Christianity. Only after I have taken the time to listen, probe a bit, and listen further have the actual issues surfaced. Then the conversation gets real.

Third, pastors need to know how people typically change their minds about things. Aristotle taught that effective rhetoric combines logos (adequate reasoning), pathos (appeal to the feelings), and ethos (an impressive persona). To this ancient wisdom, of course, Christians add the power of the Holy Spirit of God. The Spirit is the only One who can do the otherwise impossible work of converting someone's mind, yes, but also someone's *heart* to not only agree with a clever Christian argument but also embrace Jesus as Lord and Savior, to become a *disciple*.[3]

If we understand, then, that people do not typically change their minds on their first encounter with a new idea, we will not be prematurely discouraged. If we understand that different people are impressed with different sorts of evidence and argument, we will not give up when our first offering is politely (or not-so-politely) refused, but will get to know them better so as to ascertain what sort of warrant will appeal to them. If we understand that we all stick to what has worked for us in the past and exchange it for something new only when we are convinced either that the new thing is luminously better than the old or that the old is simply no longer working and we desperately need something new, then we will not be discouraged when our brilliant presentations do not result immediately in mass conversions. And if we understand that there are *spiritual* dimensions to *this* kind of change, *this* kind of conversion, then we will pray and trust God to do what only God can do in that realm.

Precisely because we do see, however, that we are partnering with God, we will not strain or push or manipulate. We will not worry that we didn't conduct the last conversation with dazzling eloquence and piercing insight. We will not approach the next one determined to tear down every defense, blast open any resistance, and jam the Good News down the ungrateful throats of—uh, oh. This is where evangelism and apologetics become ugly: when they're about me and my insecurities, rather than about my audience and their need. We are supposed to win the friend, not (just) the argument.

So we can relax. Yes, we should prepare, so that when God hands us something to do, we don't fumble the opportunity. Likewise, we should prepare our church people, for they are deployed by God throughout the community to connect with people you'll never otherwise see, let alone talk to.

But we also educate ourselves and them in *faith*: the trust that God goes before us, God is with us, and God will carry on with people long after we have left the scene. The conversation that really matters, of course, is the conversation God is having with people, not the one I (think I) am having.

Evangelizing should be as natural and as easy as possible, and many of us Christians are much too nervous. We self-censor in a way that most of our neighbors do not. If we have an observant Muslim friend and she says, "Excuse me: It's time for prayers," we oblige her without a second thought. If we have a politically active neighbor, we expect to hear about his favorite causes from time to time simply in the course of discussing life with him.

Christians should not always try to bend conversations toward spiritual things:

"Hey, did you see that great goal last night?"
"Why, yes, I did: And speaking of that, *does your life have a goal?*"

We should, however, naturally use words that convey the realities of our lives, words such as "prayer," "church," "Bible," and "Jesus." These little "religion flares" can be nicely ignored by people who want to ignore them, but they also signal a welcome to talk about such things further with those who want to do so. If we're not going to be effusive evangelists, let's at least not purge our conversation of what are in fact simply actual elements in our lives.[4]

Of course the actual elements in our lives do need to include a vital and rewarding walk with the Lord. Christians who allow themselves to run spiritually dry face the grim prospect of talking about something that lacks any experiential reality. And our audiences will know: they'll pretty quickly recognize what is in fact merely a sales pitch, rather than an actual *testimony*.

So first things first. Enjoy the gospel in your own life and help your people enjoy it in theirs. Then the evangelism and apologetics will come naturally, as we now gladly want to share this abundant life with any who will listen.

QUESTIONS FOR REFLECTION

1. What have you found to be the top three obstacles keeping people in our community from understanding or embracing the gospel?
2. Tell me a success story about a joyful sharing of the gospel in your own experience.

SUGGESTED READING

Craig, William Lane, and Chad Meister. *God Is Great, God Is Good: Why Believing in God Is Reasonable and Responsible.* Downers Grove, IL: InterVarsity Press Academic, 2009.

Plantinga, Alvin. *Knowledge and Christian Belief.* Grand Rapids, MI: Eerdmans, 2015.

Stackhouse, John G., Jr. *Can God Be Trusted? Faith and the Challenge of Evil.* Rev. ed. Downers Grove, IL: InterVarsity Press, 2009.

Stackhouse, John G., Jr. *Humble Apologetics: Defending the Faith Today.* New York and Oxford: Oxford University Press, 2005.

Williams, Clifford. *Existential Reasons for Belief in God: A Defense of Desires and Emotions for Faith.* Downers Grove, IL: InterVarsity Press Academic, 2011.

Chapter Thirteen

Engaging in Faith Formation

Sung Hee Chang

Help! Sunday school isn't working here.
Can you tell us how to revitalize it?[1]

The moment you show up as a "presumed expert" on faith formation at your field education placement, you might hear something like the soulful gospel strain, "Come rescue me, I need you right away."[2] Though the Bible has plenty of references to "it came to pass" (452 times in KJV), the speakers are grieving as they witness the passing of their beloved church education program. They simply cannot let go of it. Their credo is like Robert Fulghum's famous credo for life formation: *All I Really Need to Know I Learned in Kindergarten.* "All I really need to know I learned in *Sunday school!*" As they see it, the passing of the Sunday school era amounts to the end of faith formation in their congregation, especially for children and youth. The more you listen to stories of their "good ole days," when Sunday school classrooms were packed with students and volunteer teachers, you might be tempted to hear and feel the sentimental tune, "Hey, hey, let's make some good ole days."[3] If not this coming Sunday, then the following Sunday. Taking a sentimental approach to faith formation is the wrong path to follow.

You are not there to fix a broken system called Sunday school but to observe and learn that the golden days of this "Sunday morning dinosaur" are *already* gone.[4] You are there to help those who mourn for the passing of their "good ole days" discern what God the Good Teacher (Mark 10:17; Luke 18:18) is up to while listening to their joys and concerns. Eventually, you will note that what lingers is not only these individuals' nostalgia for a bygone era, but also their culture-specific, fragmented understanding of faith formation, which has left us with, among other things, a legacy of what is called "Sunday school syndrome." They believe that Sunday school is *a*, if

not *the*, most effective instrument for children's engagement in faith formation. They do not understand that engaging in Sunday school does not necessarily mean engaging in faith formation. According to the surprising findings
of a 2009 research project, engaging in Sunday school has done quite the
opposite: it has contributed to Sunday school children's *disengagement* from
faith formation much earlier than presumed.[5] Add to this the long-standing
criticism that faith formation in Sunday school disengages children from
critical thinking by promoting "learning without questioning,"[6] and you
come to realize that the Sunday school's problems are larger than curriculum
development, recruitment of leaders and volunteers, parental commitment,
and so forth. The problems are about *engagement in faith formation*. In short,
any issue you are asked to tackle in your field education setting cuts deeper
than you think. So when educational issues come up, ask deeper questions.

WHAT IS FAITH FORMATION?

Here are four things to keep in mind to engage meaningfully in your own
faith formation and that of people you are called to serve.

First, *it is God who ultimately forms faith*. Be wary of having a messianic
or teacher complex, as if it depends on you. Remember that just as mission is
God's mission (*missio Dei*), so education is God's education (*educatio Dei*).
No doubt faith formation involves lots of human effort, yet without divine
initiative and guidance, all the labor and toil turn out to be "vanity and a
chasing after wind" (Eccles. 1:14; 2:11). In essence, faith formation concerns
"God's Wisdom [that] engenders . . . a distinctive sort of wisdom in human
beings."[7] It is of utmost importance to engage with God in your and your
people's faith formation. And *to engage with God*, above all, means "*to seek
God's movements in every ordinary and extraordinary moment of every
day*."[8] God the Good Teacher is there to teach you and your people with
God's Wisdom, and you are the first person who needs to be taught by God.
So do not miss what John Calvin called "teachable moments."

Second, *faith formation takes the experience of context seriously*. Principally because God's Word (or Wisdom) became flesh; that is, God took
human form and lived among us (John 1:14; Phil. 2:7). This is so also
because, as Richard Osmer puts it, "formation has to do with the relationships, practices, narratives, and norms of a community's shared life."[9] According to research by the Carnegie Foundation for the Advancement of
Teaching, good teachers in theological education "approach the education of
clergy assuming that meaning and identity are always contextual, that content is hidden unless contexts become accessible to critique and open to
transformation."[10] Just as God did with God's people in the Bible, you can
engage and dialogue with your people, empowering them to respond contex-

tually to their traditions and experience. This is what contextual theology is all about. Contextual theology primarily offers the church "a new look at *itself.*"[11] Study and understand the context of your congregation or agency so that your people can see themselves in a new way through your contribution (see chapter 4, "Engaging Your Context for Ministry").

Third, it *takes a whole congregation to form faith*, just as the African proverb teaches, "it takes a whole village to raise a child." The whole congregation (and the whole agency as well) is a learning community, and "living together within the [learning] community of God's people has significant formative influence."[12] Children's Sunday school cannot and should not monopolize the vision for faith formation. Faith formation is not just for children and youth! Rather, it engages and networks all ages and generations in all aspects of life.[13] What Boyung Lee calls "a compartmentalized approach" that "alienates explicitly and implicitly related areas of ministry from each other" simply will not do. What is most needed is "a pedagogy for communal faith" that "[sees] all of the church life as the curriculum [á la Maria Harris]."[14] Engage the big picture of the congregation or agency as learning/teaching community. Ask your supervisor-mentor and education leaders in your setting, "How can we more intentionally cultivate faith-forming practices through all the events and aspects of life in our congregation or agency?"[15]

Fourth, *faith formation is not a program but a process*. The United Church of Christ has developed its educational ministries based on the following definition of faith formation: "*an engaged process of learning and practice integrated throughout all aspects of congregational and daily life.*"[16] According to Peter Hodgson, this formative process consists of three interdependent elements: (1) critical, disciplined thinking; (2) an imaginative seeing of the whole in the parts and the parts in the whole; and (3) transformative, liberating practices.[17] Do your imaginative best to include all three elements as you attempt to integrate your learning into practice and vice versa. Be aware that when faith formation engages all ages and all aspects of one's life, it also engages one's resistances and conflicts. Your supervisor-mentor will invite you to "an engaged process of naming, confronting, generating, and co-creating."[18] Consider how you can creatively invite your congregation or agency to participate in this same engaged process.

SOME PRACTICAL ADVICE REGARDING FAITH FORMATION AS AN ENGAGED PROCESS

As you are engaged in a God-initiated and guided process of communal faith formation in a particular context of a congregation or an agency, I offer my two cents' worth of counsel:

- *Be attentive to and practice the presence of God in every corner of your theological field education setting.* Brother Lawrence practiced the presence of God even "in the noise and clatter of [his] kitchen, while several persons [were] at the same time calling for different things."[19] Faith formation could happen even at a church picnic or on the gym floor. Enjoy what you have and do together in your congregation and agency, for those are God's gift (Eccles. 3:12–13).
- *Be a good listener.* As Dietrich Bonhoeffer put it, "The first service that one owes to others in the fellowship consists in listening to them." Your listening to and sharing stories of others is "a greater service than [your] speaking" to the building up of the community of faith.[20] Do not be ambitious but be humble: "Put yourself aside, and help others get ahead" (Phil. 2:3–4, The Message).
- *Develop a bible study method that weaves personal and social stories with biblical stories.* One of the major aspects of faith formation is biblical interpretation. Interpreting the Bible is the task of the community of faith. You may get some insight about this biblical pedagogical practice from Boyung Lee's "Communal Bible Study" and Eric H. F. Law's "Community Bible Study."[21] Both emphasize community building, written from a postcolonial perspective and a multicultural perspective, respectively.
- *Learn by engaging in best practices that could help you cultivate what Craig Dykstra calls "pastoral imagination,"* that is, "a set of sensibilities, virtues and skills that characteristically belongs to good pastors."[22] Theological education is all about fostering "capacities for integrating various dimensions of the educational experience" and should be practice oriented, for we learn by doing and "become what we habitually do."[23] Identify best practices in both seminary and congregational settings and practice them together with your people.
- *Take a "design" approach rather than a "nuts and bolts" approach when you deal with emerging educational problems.* Though you are involved in a very detail-oriented business called ministry, your calling is to show your people and remind them of the purpose, planning, or intention that exists behind the day-to-day operations of this mundane business, which is in fact God's business (Luke 2:49, KJV). So do not lose the forest for the trees. Create assessment opportunities for all learning activities with your leaders so that you and your people do not lose sight of God's master design.
- *Take a "team" approach toward the process of discerning what is already being done well and what is not being done well in congregational practices.* To engage in *communal* faith formation, it is very important to focus on leadership formation. It is a truism that pastors come and go and lay leaders stay. So beware of your "superman/woman syndrome" and envi-

sion the future of educational ministry together with leaders of your congregation or agency.

- *Be modest and patient with your people (as well as yourself).* Your time at this field education placement is brief. On the other hand, you are engaged in a long (perhaps lifelong) process of forming faith. God has been waiting in loving patience for God's people to learn (2 Pet. 3:9). Celebrate all that you are learning together, especially where you see growth. Until God is finally done with us, no one can say we are done with *our* faith formation.

QUESTIONS FOR REFLECTION

1. How can we "re-imagine faith formation" (John Roberto) in a way that overcomes "the enemies of personal [and communal] peace: regret over yesterday's mistakes, anxiety over tomorrow's problems and ingratitude for today's blessings" (William Arthur Ward)?
2. Ask your supervisor-mentor what has best cultivated his or her "pastoral imagination." What spiritual practices continue to nurture it in her or him?

SUGGESTED READING

Everist, Norma Cook. *The Church as Learning Community: A Comprehensive Guide to Christian Education*. Nashville, TN: Abingdon, 2002.

Harris, Maria. *Fashion Me a People: Curriculum in the Church*. Louisville, KY: Westminster John Knox, 1989.

Lee, Boyung. *Transforming Congregations through Community: Faith Formation from the Seminary to the Church*. Louisville, KY: Westminster John Knox, 2013.

Moore, Mary Elizabeth. *Teaching as a Sacramental Act*. Cleveland, OH: Pilgrim Press, 2004.

Osmer, Richard Robert. *The Teaching Ministry of Congregations*. Louisville, KY: Westminster John Knox, 2005.

Roberto, John. *Reimagining Faith Formation for the 21st Century: Engaging All Ages and Generations*. Naugatuck, CT: Lifelong Faith Associates, 2015.

Chapter Fourteen

Engaging in Church Administration

W. Joseph Mann

I remember Krister Stendahl, the great New Testament scholar and dean of Harvard Divinity School, telling us after a lecture to a campus group at North Carolina State University that he had decided to retire as dean. He said he wished to engage more fully in research, writing, and teaching. Someone in the group asked: "I guess you really are tired of all that administrative work?" Stendahl replied: "Oh, no. Any work worth doing involves administration. Administration is a gift of the Spirit."

Any work worth doing involves administration, and administration is a gift of the Spirit ("the gift of administration to administer," Rom. 12:7, Revised English Bible). At the time I heard this I was only a few years out of seminary and was serving as a campus minister at NC State University. Prior to that work I was an associate minister in a large church in Wilmington, North Carolina. In both places I learned that seminary had prepared me pretty well for most pastoral tasks and where I was lacking, I had "learned how to learn" with God's and a mentor's help. But the area that I seemed least prepared for and would indeed have to learn was administration. I had taken no course in seminary on the topic of church administration. I think there was one around, but I had no desire to be bored to death with administration when theology and Bible and all those other wonderful courses were available! I wanted to preach, observe the sacraments, be a pastor to my flock, and help the church serve the world. I certainly didn't think a course in administration would help me much. My field education experiences were mostly in pastoral care and counseling settings. I didn't even recognize that my record keeping, arranging for appointments, scheduling meetings, and working with colleagues to determine therapy regimens were all about administration.

For twenty-six years I have taught a seminary course that seeks to help students understand the dynamics of small membership churches, with an emphasis on rural churches. In that course I spend a great deal of time talking about some practical areas of leading and administering in those settings. That goes much better when the students are working in churches. They can readily see the relevance of ordering the life of a congregation within a theological context. Administrative skills are hard to teach in the abstract, but when students see the immediate relevance, talking about administration is far from boring.

In your placement you have a great opportunity to view and analyze how your supervisor-mentor practices administration and what the practices of this congregation are for ordering its life in Christ. The people of God live in time and space, and the congregation requires aid in ordering its worship, catechesis, mission, facility's needs, and financial resources. In my tradition, "Elders are authorized to preach and teach the Word, to provide pastoral care and counsel, to administer the sacraments, and *to order the life of the church* for service in mission and ministry as pastors."[1] Effectively ordering the life of the local congregation empowers the people of God to engage in ministry. Administration can mean the work that most of us don't enjoy: record keeping, data collection, and filling in report forms. But at its heart it has to do with how the church engages in the varied tasks of Word, Sacrament, Service, and Witness. Administration is holy work.

FOUR PRIORITIES IN ADMINISTRATION

I start with *ordering the life of worship and the sacraments* because that is such basic and crucial ministerial work. Pastors are entrusted with leading the people of God into worship and administering the sacraments. You likely will have limited ability to make many changes in how this congregation worships, but you can pay close attention to how it conducts and plans for worship. Observe how laypersons are involved in worship planning and leadership. You may be working with a pastor who deeply involves the laity in worship or discover that your supervisor-mentor doesn't appear to plan with or invite laity to participate greatly. Notice what the liturgies for various services are and how well the people seem to understand them.

How would you describe worship in this place: lively, engaging, and Spirit-filled? How often are the sacraments observed, especially the Eucharist? Take special pains to understand what the rules are for how this church conducts weddings, funerals, and baptisms. Are these rules the sole province of the pastor, or does the congregation know and own them as well? Ask your supervisor-mentor if you might offer a special worship service while serving there. It might be a service with one of the church groups (e.g., the women's fellowship or the youth group). How will you involve participants in the planning and leading of the worship? What will be the theme and liturgical movement? What is your role in this planning and execution? Try putting into practice ideas and skills learned in a worship course. Afterward ask participants to talk about their feelings about the worship. Take careful note what you need or want to learn during this field education opportunity or before you graduate.

Second, *observe how the congregational leaders are nurtured and sustained in their work/roles.* For a minister to order the leadership life of the church requires spending intentional relational time with members. Talk with leaders about their own Christian lives and what they are experiencing in leadership now and help them discover resources they need. Notice how your supervisor-mentor recruits, trains, and supports leaders. Try accompanying some folks not yet in leadership roles to help them discern their gifts for leadership and recruit them! You'll be helping them discover their own Christian vocation and deepen their discipleship. The administrative work of lay recruitment, training, and support really is at the heart of fruitful ministry. Volunteers are the backbone of the ministries of any congregation.

Third, note *how the programs and mission of this congregation are ordered.* We have already talked about volunteer recruitment for programs and mission; now examine how this congregation determines what programs and missions they will offer. This will mean both internal and external programs. How are current ministry commitments evaluated?

Pastors also help a congregation determine how it lives out its Christian engagement in the world. What is this congregation called by God to be and to do in its community? Clergy can help a congregation assess its God-given assets, discover the assets and needs of the community, discern where God's Spirit is already at work, and discern together what new opportunities they are called to embrace.

Imagine what you think might be done to better engage this congregation with the needs of its community or how it can grow spirituality in its internal programs. Ask your supervisor-mentor what she thinks this church does really well. Where are the challenges? What is the supervisor-mentor's vision for outreach and service programs, and what plans does she have to accomplish this? You may discern a fresh opportunity; a new Bible study for youth, a food security program to challenge the congregation to help meet the needs of the hungry around them, a prison ministry for young adults, a contemplative prayer retreat. These are ministry opportunities that will cause you to plan, recruit, implement, and review. All are administrative skills that God can and will use to help you and this congregation be the people of God where you are.

Most clergy tell me their least favorite work is the record keeping required by the congregation and/or the denomination. With all that is asked of you to perform as a minister, it's little wonder that data collection and record keeping aren't much enjoyed. And you may serve in a congregation that doesn't provide sufficient volunteer or paid staff to really manage this work. This then can become an administrative task of the first rank: how to recruit lay assistance in getting all the record keeping and reports to denominational offices done. Look around your field education placement and see who keeps attendance, finance, and other records for the church. How is your supervisor-mentor involved in all of this? This will vary by tradition and denomination. Denominational leaders often say that this sort of record keeping makes us accountable to each other. These data can help everyone see and evaluate aspects of the life of a congregation. Seeing the data can also help you determine the effectiveness of certain programs and initiatives. The philanthropic world and the church are both asking for more measurements to help determine the effectiveness of programs and to ensure good stewardship practices. You gather data and make reports to demonstrate how ministry is actually getting done.

Data collection is also needed to understand the external community. Where can you find population, economic, employment, and educational trends for the community that surrounds your church? How can you use this information to inform your mission and ministry? A good administrator certainly has a heart for ministry, but you also need to have a head for ministry. Imagine initiating a child-care program without analyzing the number of families with infants and children in your area, determining what child-care programs already exist, and considering the economic demographics in your area to help you set a fee structure that is affordable and can sustain the program. Any outreach program you do will require a similar sort of inquiry and fact gathering. Can you tell if this inquiry has occurred in this field education congregation? How well do the church and program leaders understand the effects or fruitfulness of their work? Do they have data to support their passion?

HOW WILL YOU ORDER YOUR OWN LIFE?

Fourth, how will you order your own life? I have suggested that in your field education experience you primarily examine, ask questions, and try out some practices that will help you understand the administrative duties of a minister. Let me ask you to examine yourself next. In seminary I was working in a local church and at a mental health center, and my teacher was Henri Nouwen. Henri was always worried that clergy engaged in a remarkable degree of busyness to avoid the harder inward look of prayer and silence. He challenged me to pray about the work, pray for my congregation, and listen for the voice of God in my work encounters. A good administrator doesn't just put more and more work onto the plate. Instead, clergy must learn rhythms of prayer and action all rooted in the grace of Christ. To be truly present in the work we are planning and executing will require clergy to be present with God and to see God in those serving and being served. What do you see of the devotional/prayer life of your supervisor-mentor? How does it inform his or her administrative work? A mentor of mine said that in all the churches he served, he told his church leaders that he would be unavailable between certain morning hours—time that he needed and claimed for prayer and meditation. It took a little time for folks to adjust, but they not only accepted this prayer time, they seemed to think it special that their pastor took prayer so seriously. Good administration means not just doing more work, but making sure you have the time to do the work of a spiritual leader.

You will also need to learn about yourself in the face of change, conflict, and heavy time demands placed on you. This field education experience can let you see how you react in certain situations and what makes you uncomfortable. You can learn to behave differently as you take on the mantle of authority. You also may learn what you are very comfortable with and will spend too much time doing! Learning to be a servant leader and helping order the life of a congregation requires a deep spirituality, offering yourself to Christ to be formed and shaped for the service of the Kingdom. To grow in this manner will take some intentionality and help from friends and mentors to offer love and feedback.

Woody Allen is reported to have said that 80 percent of success in life is showing up. Certainly keeping a calendar (easier done with smartphones), being on time for appointments, keeping office hours, and "showing up" are part of this success. Ordained ministry often is very lonely work, and there may be very little accountability for when and where you show up for your work. In my experience, clergy who show up at regular times so that the congregation has an idea of this availability are often rewarded! In your field education placement you may be given a set calendar with dates and times for meetings. But more likely some things will be set and much will be for you to determine. Use this experience to discover your best ways of being accountable to your parishioners and colleagues.

So you don't much like all that administrative stuff! Try in your field education to see administration through the lens of ministry. You have the authority to help order the life of the church. The Spirit gives you the gift of administration. "Let us use the different gifts allotted each of us by God's grace" (Rom. 12:6, Revised English Bible).

QUESTIONS FOR REFLECTION

1. Which of the four responsibilities in administration presents the best growth opportunity for you in this ministry context?

2. What do you owe to those whom you are directing or supporting in ministry or program leadership for them to be effective?

SUGGESTED READING

Drucker, Peter. *Managing the Non-Profit Organization: Principles and Practices*. New York: HarperCollins, 2005.

Heifetz, Ronald A., and Marty Linsky. *Leadership on the Line: Staying Alive through the Dangers of Leading*. Boston: Harvard Business Review Press, 2002.

Nouwen, Henri J. M. *In the Name of Jesus: Reflections on Christian Leadership*. Chestnut Ridge, NJ: Crossroad Publishing, 1989.

Peterson, Eugene. *Working the Angles: The Shape of Pastoral Integrity*. Grand Rapids, MI: Eerdmans, 1987.

Chapter Fifteen

Engaging for Faithful Leadership

Kyle J. A. Small

Micah completed his second sermon on Sunday as an intern at Everyone's Fine Reformed Church. Pastor Lindsay is his mentor, and he was eager to hear how she experienced his sermon. On Tuesday morning he stood at the threshold and knocked politely on her door. Pastor Lindsay looked up, smiled, and patiently said, "Good morning." Micah asked with the common anxiety of an intern seeking someone's assessment, "How did the sermon go?" Pastor Lindsay responded, "Fine. I think you did a good job. I really appreciated the exegetical work. Keep it up." Micah was underwhelmed with the response, but said a polite thank-you and quietly closed the door.

He returned to his laptop and posted his weekly discussion, as required for his field education coursework:

"I preached this past Sunday at Everyone's Fine Reformed Church. This is my second sermon, and I am really trying to assess my preaching. I wish my pastor would give me the difficult yet important coaching and evaluation I desire. I finally mustered the courage to ask my pastor, who is also my supervisor-mentor, but I left her office underwhelmed. All she could say is, 'I really appreciated the exegetical work. Keep it up.' Why is it so hard for people to give me the **feedback** *I need to grow and get better at this work?"*

LEARNING TO LEAD AS AN INTERN

Leadership practices in field education may be explored from a variety of leadership resources, including emotional intelligence,[1] Kouzes and Posner's 5 Exemplary Leadership Practices,[2] Strengths-Based Leadership,[3] the Good-to-Great fly wheel,[4] Heifetz and Linsky's adaptive practices for leading organizations,[5] and Senge's systems thinking and mental models.[6]

All of these are important and helpful for improving leadership skills, yet more central to becoming a leader is cultivating an inner depth to respond to disappointment and failure with compassion and self-differentiation. I encourage interns (also called learning leaders) to explore these aforementioned leadership skills, yet only as far as one is attending to the inner capacities of curiosity, compassion, complexity, and contemplation.[7] When it comes to engaging leadership practices in field education, learning leaders and supervisor-mentors can explore the common leadership literature within the deeper spiritual commitments of a faith community and tradition. Cultivating a spiritual depth is the primary focus of this chapter.

LEADING AS ADULT LEARNERS

Growing as a leader in the process of field education is a journey into adult learning. No longer does a syllabus or a professor determine the readings, assignments, or grading while you are out and about doing the work of field education. You're outside of the formal educational system, practicing what you want to learn. The learning is action centered, and you are the agent of the action. You're the arbiter of the experience: "What do I want to learn? What resources (people, books, conversations) do I need to engage to learn it? How will I assess my own learning?" The art of responding to these questions requires two internal abilities. Adult learners in field education must (1) be ready to learn and (2) take responsibility for learning.

Micah was ready to learn but not necessarily able to take full responsibility for his learning. He was seeking feedback. Yet Micah was asking his mentor to take an ambiguous question and make meaning of it that would satisfy him. She interpreted his question through the lens of what she *thought* he wanted. An adult learner frames the conversation in such a way as to help the respondent answer the learner's question. This takes skill, maturity, and patience in forming and asking the question.

Taking responsibility for learning through asking for feedback is often a scary and difficult task. One of the hurdles to becoming an adult learner is a series of anxiety-driven triggers: "What if I fail? What if I ask for help and am rejected? What if I seek evaluation from peers and mentors and they criticize me? What happens if I am asking the wrong questions?" The paralyzing effect of learner anxiety is real. Yet the movement from student to leader via adult learner is a competency necessary for engaging the fullness of theological field education.

READINESS AND RESPONSIBILITY FOR FEEDBACK

You're not alone. The fears of adult learning plague intern and mentor alike. The paralyzing feelings within an intern *and* a mentor generate discomfort with honesty and with tension and resistance. Honesty, tension, and resistance are necessary for a learning environment. The discomfort can lead to passivity or worse, being nice. There are too few hours in a week and too much anxiety in raising difficult conversations around an intern's performance, disposition, and impact. I do not know of a supervisor-mentor who wants to disrupt an intern's journey or participate in an intern's undoing through misunderstood feedback.

You can develop leadership skills and cultivate spiritual depth through the difficult practice of learning to receive feedback. Seeking feedback is a spiritual quest that lives at the intersection of two desires: "our drive to learn and our longing for acceptance."[8] The quest is to know how to ask for feedback, from whom, and for what purpose. Micah asked for feedback, but in the ambiguity of his question, the pastor offered him evaluation, albeit *nice* and largely disconnected from what he wanted to receive. The problem is not Pastor Lindsay's response but Micah's limitations in asking for feedback. This is a common problem in field education (and in most vocational environments).

Adult learners "create pull" and develop a growth mentality by taking a risk and asking for specific feedback with specific intentions and outcomes.[9] Learning leaders desire to know how, when, and whom to ask for feedback. Affirmation, coaching, and evaluation are three forms of feedback, and we need all three.[10] Each has its time and place depending on what the learning leader needs and desires. Learning covenants are excellent means to prioritize and ask for the kind of feedback you desire during the internship. Engaging with peers is an additional way to practice asking for different kinds of feedback.

GETTING TO THE HEART OF LEADING

The central leadership practice in receiving feedback is cultivating a growth identity.[11] In theological field education this includes remembering our baptism and how identity is rooted in God and *not* in our accomplishments, our failures, or our judgments. Christian leadership develops through a process of spiritual formation toward depth and contemplation. In the Office of Formation for Ministry at Western Theological Seminary, we often say that a growth identity forms as one increases in curiosity, complexity, compassion, and contemplation.

One congregational example of this work occurred at the Church of the Saviour in Washington, D.C., under the leadership of Gordon Cosby. Membership at Church of the Saviour included practicing centering prayer daily and participating in a spiritual direction group exploring call, vocation, leadership, and mission weekly. Church of the Saviour taught me that learning to lead comes from an internal depth that seeks to love the world with curiosity and compassion and through complexity and contemplation. I believe that nonreligious leadership publications are recognizing the necessity for these same habits and will look to religion and spirituality for the deeper practices of leadership in the years ahead.

A LIFELONG LEARNING LEADER

Wesley Granberg-Michaelson is one mature leader who experienced the formation of Church of the Saviour. Granberg-Michaelson is a former general secretary of the Reformed Church in America and founder of Christian Churches Together. He tells his story of becoming a learning leader who is able to receive coaching and evaluation as an act of leadership and spiritual formation. This ability was learned through contemplation.

Wesley was mentored by Gordon Cosby. Pastor Cosby interfered with Wesley early in his formation: "You will have many opportunities. The question will not be if you are able, for you have the skills and ability. The question is whether you will be ready, in terms of your inner journey and spiritual and psychological integration, to discern God's call and to freely embrace and fulfill it?"[12] This kind of feedback is rare but life shaping. This is feedback that doesn't simply applaud but looks deep into the soul and calls forth faithfulness. Wesley has carried this with him for decades. You must learn to stay present to difficult feedback, and even more, to seek it from trusted and wise mentors.

LEADING FROM DEPTH AND FEEDBACK

Micah returned to the threshold of Pastor Lindsay's office several weeks later and asked to enter. He sat down across from her desk. The night before Micah had led the deacons' meeting, in which they discussed how to organize and communicate the upcoming World Relief offering. Thankfully, Pastor Lindsay had participated in the meeting and was able to observe his leadership. Micah noticed the compassion in his mentor's eyes, so he quickly blurted out, "Anything you want to say about the meeting last night?" He caught himself asking a vague question and halted his mentor before she could answer. He took a deep breath, remembered where he was and why, and started again. "Pastor Lindsay, I want to be better at leading meetings.

Specifically, I struggle to know how to lead a meeting that places spiritual depth with agenda management. I would be grateful to have a conversation with you on (1) how you integrate meetings as discipleship and (2) how you experienced me doing this work last night." The conversation ensued on the intersection of leadership and discipleship. The mentor and intern became learning leaders with one another.

Micah returned to his office and sat down to post his weekly discussion:

I practiced my desire to learn today. I reengaged with my mentor on feedback. She participated in a meeting I led with the deacons yesterday evening. I really wanted to know from her how I did. Initially, I wanted her to tell me how great I am and that she thinks I can be a good leader. However, upon deeper thought, I took a step back and breathed deeply like we are learning through contemplative/centering prayer. I could feel the clarity in my mind and body. I asked her a specific and clear question on how to lead a meeting with spiritual depth and task focus. We spent ninety minutes together. She shared authentically and vulnerably about the challenges of holding the two together. She values honoring people's time but also recognizes how difficult cultivating discipleship is for laity and clergy alike, especially when the setting is labeled a "meeting." Even when she feels time pressure, she begins every meeting with a collaborative prayer or Scripture exercise that invites God into the conversation and expects everyone to "show up."

She asked me how I felt and thought about how I began the meeting last night. Too often, I feel the rush to get on with the meeting, so I quickly and fervently pray and insert something into the prayer that relates to how I think the meeting ought to go. I did this last night.

My mentor noticed my anxiety and asked me to share what I thought made me anxious. I responded, "The conversation was difficult for me—I knew we were talking about money and ministry; money scares me, and I was afraid I might say something that would make people feel guilty or ashamed about the upcoming generosity campaign." She then mentioned how prayer can become benign manipulation, pseudo-spiritual filler, or performance in times like that.

Pastor Lindsay encouraged me to borrow a spiritual discipline that I can continually invite lay members to practice at the beginning of each meeting. I think I will borrow her Scripture reading practice; I am not sure if I have the confidence to teach them centering prayer yet.

QUESTIONS FOR REFLECTION

1. How do you feel when someone begins to offer you feedback following a leadership experience? If you feel anxious, practice connecting your mind, heart, and body through deep and slow breathing. This is

an act of prayer. How does it feel to hear someone's coaching or evaluation now?

2. Who is someone (one step beyond your comfort zone) whom you can ask for coaching and evaluation feedback? Seek out that person, invite him or her to experience you leading, and develop a coaching or evaluation question to ask that person.

SUGGESTED READING

Heifetz, Ronald, Alexander Grashow, and Martin Linsky. *Practice of Adaptive Leadership*. Boston: Harvard Business Press, 2009.

Kouzes, James, and Barry Posner. *The Leadership Challenge*. San Francisco: Jossey-Bass, 2002.

Merton, Thomas. *New Seeds of Contemplation*. New York: New Directions, 1961.

Senge, Peter. *The Fifth Discipline: The Art and Practice of the Learning Organization*. New York: Doubleday, 1990.

Stone, Douglas, and Sheila Heen. *Thanks for the Feedback: The Science and Art of Receiving Feedback Well*. New York: Viking, 2014.

Chapter Sixteen

Engaging in Public Ministry

David W. Watkins, III

Wow! You're here. I am excited for you and this journey that you are on. You are intentionally exploring God's calling and vocation for your life. You are expanding your leadership skills. Collectively, this journey of exploration, expansion, and experience will shape your pastoral identity and inform your pastoral practice for years to come.

But wait! You want to do what? Challenge the status quo? Dismantle systems of oppression, white supremacy, and racism? Fight injustice? Participate in the #BlackLivesMatter movement? Are you sure about this? Do you really want to make this world a better place to live, work, and play? Yes, this is the work of engaging social justice.

Engaging in social justice ministry is a high calling from God. I hope to stimulate your thoughts, stir your reflections, and strengthen your resolve to engage in social justice during your field education journey. Like the prophet Isaiah, maybe you will hear the voice of the Lord saying, *"Whom shall I send, and who will go for us"* and you will answer *"Here am I; send me!"* (Isa. 6:8).

WHAT IS SOCIAL JUSTICE, AND WHY DOES IT MATTER?

Social justice has been defined in numerous ways. My working definition is the visionary pursuit of a just, equitable society in which all people can flourish with dignity, respect, and equality so that our life in community together is enhanced. How would you define it?

Engaging in social justice has a long history within numerous faith traditions. It is the public faith leadership of Aung San Suu Kyi (Buddhist), Malcolm X (Muslim), Dietrich Bonhoeffer (Lutheran), Martin Luther King

Jr. (Baptist), Óscar Romero (Roman Catholic), Mohandas Gandhi (Hindu), and many other women and men of faith.[1]

I believe that *engaging in social justice is a crucial, yet often neglected, aspect of the call and vocation of clergy and congregations of Jesus Christ.* Don't say it; I know. Many disagree with me. Some argue that clergy and congregations are called to save souls, baptize converts, celebrate the Lord's Supper, care for the sick, marry couples, bless babies, and bury saints. I totally agree. However, I vehemently disagree that the priestly and pastoral functions are the only roles to which clergy and congregations are called. I contend that failing to confront injustice and address complex social issues from a biblical and theological perspective is *biblical/theological treason* and *ecclesiastical malpractice.*

To reduce the gospel ministry to the "saving of souls" and the "proper performance of ritual" is to minimize the incarnation of God in Christ and to be derelict in duty concerning the very people Jesus identified himself with: the hungry, the naked, the sick, the stranger, and the imprisoned (Matt. 25:31–46). In his inaugural sermon for public faith leadership, Jesus declared his pastoral identity and pastoral practice to be that of a prophet: a public faith leader who uses his or her position and voice to seek justice for the poor, the oppressed, and the marginalized of society (Luke 4:16–18). Theologically, social justice is a means of embodying the Great Commandments to "love God and love neighbor" as witness to God's unlimited love for all people. Therefore, engaging in this work is a nonnegotiable priority for clergy and congregations.

PRACTICAL CONSIDERATIONS

What then are best practices for engaging in public faith leadership? Here are four practical considerations, summarized by the acronym LEAD:

- **L**isten deeply.
- **E**xamine critically.
- **A**ct justly.
- **D**evelop spiritually.

Listen Deeply

First and fundamentally, engaging in social justice begins with listening deeply. Whether your congregation is located in an urban, suburban, rural, or small town, the issues of racism, poverty, poor education, and the environment (just to name a few) are alive and in need of attention. Acquire firsthand knowledge by immersing yourself in the flow of the community while bathing it all in prayer. Show up at community meetings. Participate in the block club. Eavesdrop on conversations at the local grocery store, coffee shop, farmers' market, playground, and other public spaces. Walk the neighborhood. Engage all of your senses. Hear, see, smell, and feel what community members deal with every day. What do you smell? What is happening in the lives of residents? What is the spirit of this community? What values emerge? What types of institutions and businesses are located here? Who else is present? Who is missing? What makes this community tick? What communal concerns surface? Record your observations and your questions. You can learn a lot about a neighborhood just by being present.

The second part of listening deeply involves being curious. Target three to five influential leaders in the community. Begin with your supervisor-mentor and congregational leaders. Ask them: "What are the most pressing needs in the community? What does the congregation have to say about said needs?" Consider meeting with a school principal, social service director, business owner, other clergy, an elected official, a judge, or a police superintendent. Be a good journalist—ask good questions! Useful guides/templates for being curious include strengths, weaknesses, opportunities, threats (SWOT) analysis; asset-based community development (ABCD) questionnaires, and the appreciative inquiry (AI) method. Dig deep. Get the leaders' perspectives on the joys and injustices in the community. Ask for additional contacts. Not only will you receive good information, you are also laying the building blocks for strong relationships to engage this work.

Don't stop there! Influential leaders are often sought out for their voices. In fact, we hear their voices all the time. You have the opportunity to do something different, something transformative. Be courageous. Seek the voices of the unheard. Too often, their voices go unheard in school board meetings, in legislative chambers, and within the justice system. By focusing on the voices of the unheard, you can gain a deeper appreciation of the real impact that injustice has on real people: the working poor, the immigrant, the child traumatized by violence.

Transformative education happens not only in the hallowed halls of the seminary but also through holy, sacred conversations in the streets. Risk being ignorant! Social justice insists learning *from*, not just learning *about*. Learn from the life experiences of others. Risk having uncomfortable (*yes, old-fashioned, face-to-face*) conversations about race, gender, sexual orientation, and privilege. Share your perspective honestly. Risk being misunderstood. Allow your own assumptions, views, and perspectives about social conditions and systemic injustice to be challenged. Allow "the least of these" to shape and form you. This is how trust is earned. Like Jesus, build solidarity with "the least of these." Eat with them. Laugh with them. Cry with them. Dream with them. Embrace them. Cultivate transformative relationships with them. Remember, God is present!

If you take the risk, you will experience what Rev. Dr. Martin Luther King Jr. once said, "*I am cognizant of the interrelatedness of all communities and states. . . . Injustice anywhere is a threat to justice everywhere. We are caught in an inescapable network of mutuality, tied in a single garment of destiny. Whatever affects one directly affects all indirectly.*"[2] To do the work of social justice, we must invest ourselves and build relationships in the community where we serve by listening deeply. Be present. Be curious. Be courageous. This is solidarity for justice.

Examine Critically

Engage social justice through critical examination. As Nehemiah engaged community and listened deeply, he clearly identified one concrete issue of injustice to work on: "*The wall of Jerusalem is broken down*" (Neh. 1:4). Likewise, I encourage you to pray fervently (cf. Neh. 1:5 11) and ask for clarity. What issue of injustice concerns you and the congregation? Identify it, describe it, and learn all you can about it.

You already have considerable skill for engaging this task. You have been taught how to exegete texts, research issues, think critically, analyze and critique arguments, make correlations, and draw your own conclusions. These tools in your toolbox will come in handy. To uncover and address the root causes of systemic injustice, apply these transferable skills to examine the historical, structural, and societal aspects of the injustice you identify:[3]

- **Historical**—Probe the deep background influences of the past on the present. What is the main line of history of this injustice? What are the key turning points? Identify major events. What patterns emerge?
- **Structural**—What are the major *economic*, *political*, and *cultural* structures that determine how resources are distributed, how power is organized, and how meaning is made? These structures are interrelated and form systems. Systems are perfectly designed to achieve the results they are achieving.[4] One of the best tools is the power analysis exercise used in community organizing.
- **Societal**—Examine injustices through the lens of societal divisions, including race, gender, age, class, ethnicity, religion, sexual orientation, geography, and so forth. It is critical to collect data, because the impact of a particular event or injustice does not affect all people in the same way (e.g., economic recession, war on drugs, urban violence).

To this list, I encourage you to add the *legal* aspects of injustice. Please do not confuse law and justice. Just because a statute is legal does not mean it is just. By definition and discrimination, the marginalized and oppressed are not in positions of power to pass the laws, write the policies, and create the systems that often and disproportionately impact them negatively.

Finally, as a public faith leader you must also examine injustice theologically. Employ your biblical insights, theological training, pastoral instincts, and prophetic witness to the issue at hand. Is there a "word from the Lord?" What passages of scripture come to mind? How does this injustice inform your theology of sin? The human condition? Redemption? Christology? Be open to entertain opposing perspectives and theologies. Your examination is incomplete until you do so. Share your research and reflections with your supervisor-mentor. Engage in rigorous reflection together. By examining injustice theologically, soon you will speak as a distinctive, prophetic, justice-oriented voice.

Act Justly

After listening deeply and examining critically, it is time to act, right? Yes, but not so fast. Let's begin with an observation. In Micah 6:8 God, through the prophet, calls people of faith to "do justice" and "love mercy." While justice and mercy are related concepts, they are not the same type of activity.

In general, social justice–related activities fall on a continuum between charity (love mercy) and justice (activism). While charity and activism are essential to the call and vocation of clergy and congregations, "an exclusive focus on charity impedes progress towards justice."[5] Why? As you consider power dynamics, charity accepts the existing oppressive power structures, while activism seeks to transform power structures for the common good.

As you prayerfully consider goals for your learning serving covenant, consult table 16.1. How will you act?

Before acting justly, there's one more thing. Social justice ministry is a team sport. Engaging social justice demands that we work collaboratively to act justly. Activists in Chicago embody the slogan "Teamwork Makes the Dream Work!" The arduous work of justice must not (and cannot) be done alone. Make critical connections. Meet together. Strategize together. Plan together. Work together. Participate in God's work to transform this world into a place where all people can flourish with dignity, respect, and equality.

Develop Spiritually

In Micah 6:8, the call to do justice and love mercy concludes with "walk humbly with God." The Hebrew verb "to walk humbly" literally means "to live or behave in a modest manner" in God's presence. To adapt a phrase from theologian Rev. Brad R. Braxton, social justice working must be connected to sanctified walking. Braxton challenges our seeking justice over seeking Jesus:

2

Table 16.1.   Continuum of Social Justice–Related Activities

Related Activity	Definition	Examples
Charity (i.e., direct or social service)	Providing temporary aid/assistance for those in need	Soup kitchens, prison ministry, food pantry, clothing drive, prayer vigils
Education	Learning about issues, identifying resources, raising the awareness of others	HIV/AIDS summit, home ownership forums, job readiness training
Politics	Engaging the political process to advance issues of justice, rights, equality within the current power structure	Range of activities: hosting candidate forums, voter registration drives, holding public office (e.g., serving on local school boards, in town/city/state/national government)
Advocacy	Speaking "truth to power" to promote changes in legislation, policies, funding for the common good	Providing safe sanctuary for immigrants, lobbying legislators for affordable health care, letter-writing campaigns
Activism	Direct action, often led by those marginalized, to bring about permanent structural, political, and social change	Community organizing around pressing issue(s), civil disobedience (e.g., rallies, die-ins, protests)

Sources: Diane C. Olson and Laura Dean F. Friedrich, *Weaving a Just Future for Children: An Advocacy Guide* (Nashville, TN: Discipleship Resources, 2008); Danielle L. Ayers and Reginald W. Williams Jr., *To Serve This Present Age: Social Justice Ministries in the Black Church* (Valley Forge, PA: Judson Press, 2013); and Edward T. Chambers, *Roots for Radicals: Organizing for Power, Action, and Justice* (New York: Bloomsbury Academic, 2010).

> Can the same be said of many preachers? A master of divinity degree, required for ordained ministry in many Christian traditions, does not necessarily ensure a sanctified life. . . . "*It is possible to have a master of divinity without being in relationship with the Master of Divinity. . . .* [B]y pursuing a vibrant spiritual life, we ensure that God has the sharpest tools with which to work.[6]

During your field experience, I encourage you to include a spiritual development goal in your learning-serving convent to find ways to *rest, reconnect,* and *reflect.* Engaging in social justice with faithfulness, integrity, and longevity requires a deep spirituality (see chapter 7).

I am convinced that social justice as a ministry focus area is a bona fide high calling from God. I am further convinced that authentic, life-transforming experiences begin with a willingness to take risks and be vulnerable. Stretch beyond your comfort zone! Take the risk! Go! Push beyond the comfort zone and LEAD.

QUESTIONS FOR REFLECTION

1. As you engage the community in your field education placement, what do you feel? What saddens you? What surprises you?
2. On the social justice–related continuum, which area resonates with you? Which makes you most uncomfortable? Why?
3. What devotional practices do you currently engage in to sustain vitality and effectiveness in ministry?

SUGGESTED READING

Ayers, Danielle L., and Reginald W. Williams Jr. *To Serve This Present Age: Social Justice Ministries in the Black Church*. Valley Forge, PA: Judson Press, 2013.

Chambers, Edward T. *Roots for Radicals: Organizing for Power, Action, and Justice*. New York: Bloomsbury Academic, 2010.

DeYoung, Curtiss Paul. *Living Faith: How Faith Inspires Social Justice*. Minneapolis, MN: Fortress Press, 2007, Kindle e-book.

McMickle, Marvin A. *Pulpit and Politics: Separation of Church and State in the Black Church*. Valley Forge, PA: Judson Press, 2014.

Olson, Diane C., and Laura Dean F. Friedrich. *Weaving a Just Future for Children: An Advocacy Guide*. Nashville, TN: Discipleship Resources, 2008.

Stroh, David P. *Systems Thinking for Social Change: A Practical Guide to Solving Complex Problems, Avoiding Unintended Consequences, and Achieving Lasting Results*. White River Junction, VT: Chelsea Green Publishing, 2015.

Chapter Seventeen

Engaging Learning Across Generations

Nathan E. Kirkpatrick

In my first field education placement, during my first committee meeting, I said something that betrayed both my inexperience and my impatience with statements like "but we've always done it this way." I forget what I said, but I remember the reaction. One person on the committee turned to me and asked bluntly, "Where were you when Kennedy was shot or when Nixon resigned or when my brother was killed in Vietnam? Where were you? That's right, you weren't born yet. Where was I? I came to this church when those things happened. I. Was. Here."

Kind? Not really. Memorable? Certainly. Humbling? Absolutely.

It was my own Job 38 moment. You remember God thundering out of the whirlwind at Job, chiding him for his pride? "Where were you when I laid the foundation of the earth? Tell me, if you have understanding. Who determined its measurements—surely you know! Or who stretched the line upon it?" (Job 38:4–5).

Where was I? I hadn't been born yet. Where was she? She had come to the church—that church—and had taken solace and comfort in being at prayer with her community of faith. In her "question," she named that there was a generational gap between us, and it became clear to me that I would have to bridge that gap if I was to be in ministry to and with her.

ONE OF THE LAST INTERGENERATIONAL PLACES

It is frequently observed that churches are one of the last truly intergenerational places in American society. This is often a gift to the church. It gives us a wealth and depth of wisdom; it gives us a diversity of experiences and perspectives that can prove instructive. If we listen to the stories that get told

in congregations, we can hear of God's enduring faithfulness across generations. We can find countless examples of the way that the Spirit enables the
resilience of the church even against incredible odds. The intergenerational
nature of the church can shore up our faith, confirm our hope, and enliven
our witness.

But the church's intergenerational nature presents some clear challenges
for our life together and for our practice of ministry. Different generations
can have different theological understandings of the mission of the church
and whom the church exists to serve. They can have different priorities for
the work of ministry that reflect both differing visions of what it means to be
a minister and the unique spiritual needs of a particular generation at a
particular point in time. Furthermore, generations may not share the same
sense of what membership or commitment means, which can lead to dis-
agreements, unfulfilled expectations, and resentments within the congregation.

On a smaller scale but no less important, different generations have different understandings of what is considered "professionally appropriate,"
understandings that can both positively and negatively shape ministry.
Across the generations active in today's church, people answer questions like
"what should the minister wear" or "when should the minister be in the
office" or "when should the minister be available by phone or e-mail" or
even "what is the purpose of a meeting" in surprisingly different ways, and as
a ministerial intern, you will have to navigate these stated and unstated
expectations to the best of your ability.

This is good practice for a life spent in lay or ordained ministry. Part of
what you will be learning in your field education placement is how to receive
the gifts that come with the intergenerational nature of the church, while at
the same time working to overcome the challenges inherent within it. While
I've been speaking principally about the church, if you're called to serve in
the nonprofit sector or the academy, you'll face similar opportunities and
challenges.

HOW BEST TO ENGAGE GENERATIONAL DIFFERENCE

First, *bring your best communication skills.* While this is important in all
aspects of ministry, when bridging generational differences, your ability to
speak clearly from the heart of who you are, to listen deeply to another
person, and to help others listen deeply to each other matters all the more.
You will want to model using "I" statements ("I feel . . . ," "I believe . . . ,"
"in my experience . . ."), rather than using "we" or "they" statements ("we all
know that . . . ," "they believe that . . . ," "you all seem . . ."). Using these
kinds of "I" statements will require self-awareness and critical reflection on

your part. In addition, you will want to ask open-ended questions, the kind that encourage self-reflection and story sharing rather than questions that are too easily brushed off with a "yes" or a "no." Remember that the aim of every encounter is, as St. Francis reminds us, first to understand the other person before seeking to be understood by him.

Second, *listen for values*. As you are employing your best communication skills in your internship setting, you will want to listen for what is not being said but what is nonetheless being expressed—the articulation of values. Often when we find ourselves pinched between generations in a congregational discussion or disagreement, what we are experiencing is a conflict of values or priorities. So listen for what matters to people. Pay attention to visual cues, too (What pictures do they have? How do your coworkers in ministry decorate their offices?). Your capacity to perceive and articulate values is an essential gift if people are to be able to hear one another and ultimately find common ground.

In that same first field education placement, I remember a parishioner declaring in a meeting, "You know what the Good Book says, right? 'The church is the same yesterday, today, and forever.'" He almost got it right (remember, according to the writer of Hebrews, it's Jesus who is the same yesterday, today, and forever), but what you hear in what this Traditionalist (a member of the generation born before 1945) was saying is a valuing of the reliability of institutions. Change in the church was threatening to him because it meant that an institution he cared about might not be durable or lasting in a form he recognized. My field education supervisor-mentor said as much to him in a gentle pastoral way, and that allowed him to moderate his previously strident position on the matter before the congregational council.

Third, *harvest wisdom*. Resident within each congregation, there is a hard-fought, hard-won wisdom about what it means to be a community of faith. Resident within each pastor and ministry professional, there is wisdom about what it means to lead a community of faith. And resident within each parishioner, there is wisdom about what it means to be a person of faith. Yet often this wisdom is not shared without the opportunity to do so. Your presence can allow people to articulate things that they know but that they have never said before. You can be a catalyst for cross-generational wisdom sharing.

Often this cross-generational wisdom sharing will come through feedback you receive, some of which you will appreciate and some of which you will resist. It can be easy to dismiss feedback that sounds inspired by generational preferences ("you should really wear a suit or dress if you're going to be a preacher" or "*that* music isn't appropriate in divine worship" or "you shouldn't have your headphones in your ears while you're in the church office"), but if you listen to the feedback and ask clarifying questions about it, you will find wisdom that's worth treasuring in it. (What is it about a suit or dress that conveys authority and respect to a person? Why is some music considered by this congregation to be sacred and other music not? What does multitasking in ministry convey to those you are sent to serve?)

Fourth, *keep in mind the complex events that have shaped a generation's worldview*. Every year, Wisconsin's Beloit College publishes its "Mindset List," a list of things that have somehow defined reality for that year's incoming freshman class. In past years the list has included things like "[for this entering class,] the Soviet Union has never existed and therefore is about as scary as the student union" (Class of 2010); "caller ID has always been available on phones" (Class of 2012); "[t]wo-term presidents are routine, but none of them ever won in a landslide" (Class of 2018).

While Beloit's list is year to year, we can imagine a list that is generation to generation. For Traditionalists, we would need to include experiences like the Great Depression, World War II, 1950s suburbia, and the baby boom. For baby boomers (those born 1946–1964), we should note generation-shaping experiences like the Cold War, the Kennedy assassination, the civil rights movement and the murder of Martin Luther King Jr., and the Vietnam War. For Gen X (those born 1965–1980), we should remember the space shuttle *Challenger* explosion, the Rodney King beating and the riots that followed, the Gulf War, the Clarence Thomas–Anita Hill hearings, and the Clinton impeachment. For Millennials (those born 1981–2001), the influence of the terrorist attacks on September 11, 2001, and the subsequent War on Terror, the economic downturn of the late 2000s, and technology cannot be overstated. Each of these events, and others we might name, has shaped the mind-set and worldview of entire generations.

In the church there are other significant events that have shaped "generational" mind-sets. Within denominations there are clear generational fault lines. There will be those who lived through debates about the participation of women in ordained ministry, and there will be women who were the first to serve, many of whom did so in hostile environments. There will be those who have endured denominational fights over questions of lesbian, gay, bisexual, transgender, and queer (LGBTQ) inclusion, and there will be LGBTQ persons who know what it is like to have their identity debated before them. These will become "generations" within denominations, even as there will be those who come after these questions have been answered who will wonder why they were ever questions.

Likewise, within a local congregation, an experience of pastoral or lay misconduct, a pastoral transition deftly or poorly handled, a season of profound growth or decline, the addition of a building, or a community tragedy will form and shape congregational "generations." Within the congregation there will be people who predate the experience and people who come after who have no memory of it and little understanding of why it matters.

As a ministerial intern, you will want to keep these generational lines in mind even as you work to bridge the divides that they represent.

Fifth, *continue learning about generational differences.* There are many good books written on the subject, and they can help you understand why Traditionalists come to church (even to the contemporary worship service) in a coat and tie, why baby boomers will always ask you for a meeting, why Gen Xers will respect you once you've earned it, and why Millennials have no patience for the voicemail you just left them (text them, please!).

In your reading and learning about generations, though, remember that it is possible to make too much of generational differences. Generational categories are meant to be descriptive, not predictive, and not every difference between generations causes disagreement or disaster. So it is dangerous to begin a relationship with a parishioner (or your supervisor-mentor) assuming that because a person belongs to a certain generation, he or she will behave or believe in a certain way. We share a great deal across generations, and even when we do have substantive differences, the Spirit still works, sometimes leading people beyond their own preferences and predispositions. We must give the Spirit some room to surprise.

Finally, *remember that your presence in a congregational internship represents hope.* Whether you understand your calling to be to ordained ministry or not, your presence during your internship communicates that communities of faith and the people who belong to them matter. Your presence says that God *is* raising up a new generation of leaders—lay and ordained—to serve the people of God. All is not lost, and that is worth celebrating.

But a word of caution: in some denominations, the presence of your generation of new leaders is so exciting that you will be loved too much. There will be too much hope and too many expectations put on your shoulders. ("Young clergy will save the church!") Denominational leaders may fetishize you, and congregational leaders with longer tenures may come to resent you or the opportunities afforded to you. This is a new generational divide within the church, and we will need your help to bridge it.

Remind us that every Samuel has needed an Eli, and every Eli has waited for a Samuel.

QUESTIONS FOR REFLECTION

1. How many generations are represented within this congregation? Are the generations evenly distributed, or does one dominate? How does that impact the church's ministry and your ministry priorities?
2. Which generation is easiest for you to relate to? Why do you think that is?

3. What do you hope I learn about the intergenerational nature of the church during my internship?

SUGGESTED READING

Hamman, Jaco. *Becoming a Pastor: Forming Self and Soul for Ministry*. 2nd ed. Cleveland, OH: Pilgrim Press, 2014, esp. 143–146.

Shaw, Haydn. *Generational IQ: Christianity Isn't Dying, Millennials Aren't the Problem, and the Future Is Bright*. Carol Stream, IL: Tyndale, 2015.

Shaw, Haydn. *Sticking Points: How to Get 4 Generations Working Together in the 12 Places They Come Apart*. Carol Stream, IL: Tyndale, 2013.

Chapter Eighteen

Engaging as a Gendered Person

Kimberly L. Clayton

O how careful we ought to be, lest through our by-laws of church government and discipline, we bring into disrepute even the word of life. For as unseemly as it may appear now-a-days for a woman to preach, it should be remembered that nothing is impossible with God. And why should it be thought impossible, heterodox, or improper, for a woman to preach? seeing the Saviour died for the woman as well as the man.

If a man may preach, because the Saviour died for him, why not the woman? seeing he died for her also. Is he not a whole Saviour, instead of a half one? as those who hold it wrong for a woman to preach, would seem to make it appear.

—Jarena Lee, 1833 [1]

It's nothing *personal*, Kim, I just don't think women ought to be ministers.
—Member, Presbyterian Church in Georgia, to me as a seminary intern, 1983

Sometimes we forget how great it is to be a woman in the church. Once a young girl from the congregation ran up to me after the service and said, with this huge grin, "I didn't know girls could do that!" That just made my day.
—Pastor, 2011 [2]

"So God created humankind in his image, in the image of God he created them; male and female God created them" (Gen. 1:27).

Genesis 1 seems clear and straightforward, but we are learning how complex "gender" is, and "that human nature is more variable, even more mysterious, than we had once assumed. Ongoing research—physiological and psychological—confirms that gender is experienced along a wide spectrum." James and Evelyn Whitehead invite us to see the diversity regarding gender expressions as "a signature feature of creation—God's extravagance"[3] rather than a source of concern. Yet culturally and religiously, we remain more comfortable with settled, delineated norms and expectations of what is "male"/masculine and "female"/feminine. Gender typically refers to social and cultural differences, not biological ones. It encompasses social and cultural norms and expectations assigned to men and women. Men have been the pastors (and in some denominations being biologically male is still a requirement), but women also occupy this role in increasing numbers where church tradition and law allow it. In some denominations, people who are gender nonconforming or who are transgender also serve as pastors.

As you enter your theological field education placement, you may become conscious of what it means to be a "gendered person" in ways you never imagined. In this role you will experiment with and begin to form your sense of pastoral identity. Like putting on a preaching robe or clerical collar for the first time, you will be "trying on" pastoral authority to see how it "fits" you, how you *embody* it. Gender norms and expectations can affect you consciously and unconsciously, impacting how you perceive yourself as a pastor. These same norms and expectations can also affect how others perceive and experience you in a pastoral role. Internal reflection and external feedback from others (solicited and unsolicited!) can elicit many emotions, especially when your gender becomes the focus of attention. You may feel affirmed, challenged, irritated, delighted, bemused, even amused— sometimes all at once! A supervisor who can discuss the ways gender impacts the practice of ministry will be of great benefit.

Male pastors have been the defining "norm" in religious communities and in cultural images. Just as "whiteness" in American culture has been determinative, leading to inequity, injustice, and presumptive attitudes, so "maleness" has been determinative in the church across the centuries. It is so deeply ingrained that when a woman preaches or conducts a wedding, she may be seen as "other," an "alternative" because she does not fit the stereotype of pastor in those settings. Along with visual images, the words we use have power to shape what is normal and acceptable. But language also has power to transform the way we understand and engage the world, the church, around us. When gender-inclusive language is used for God and human beings in worship, education, and even committee meetings, new possibilities open up for all people to be acknowledged and affirmed.

The quotes that opened this chapter attest that women have always had to "engage gender" when responding to God's call to ministry. I entered seminary as a young woman over thirty years ago, joining a class of fifty-five men and five women. The women often had difficulty finding a church that would welcome them for a seminary internship, and it was harder still to find ordained positions upon graduation. Though my denomination, the Presbyterian Church (U.S.A.), recently celebrated sixty years of women's ordination as pastors, women remain underrepresented as senior or solo pastors in our larger congregations. Clergywomen, in denominations that allow women to serve as clergy, more often serve as associate pastors, as chaplains in other ministry settings, and as pastors of smaller congregations. Of course, steady strides have been made over the decades for women seeking to serve the church in positions of leadership.[4] Approximately one in five Protestant seminary students is a woman, and around 8 to 10 percent of congregations have a woman in senior or solo leadership (20 percent for mainline Protestant churches). Yet the national pay gap that affects women across professions (women earn 83 cents for every dollar men make) is even worse for female clergy, who earn 76 cents for every dollar that male clergy earn—a gap that *widens* with experience.[5]

"Therefore I tell you, do not worry about your life, what you will eat or what you will drink, or about your body, what you will wear. Is not life more than food, and the body more than clothing?" (Matt. 6:25).

Then again, Jesus never had to be a seminary intern. If your supervisor went to seminary many years ago, he or she likely had very specific instruction, even requirements, regarding clergy dress. Men would have been counseled to wear suits and ties in darker hues, dark socks, and dark shoes. Women received the same advice about the clergy color palette—black was the safest choice; navy blue if you dared. But for women, there was more: dresses and skirts, pantyhose, and closed-toed shoes (black, of course, with modest heels) were the norm. Necklines should not be too low nor hemlines too high. No dangly or sparkly earrings. Hair should be styled tastefully, and no red lipstick! The rationale, in keeping with our Reformed heritage, was that nothing should distract from the true focus of worship: the glory of God and the Word read and proclaimed. We were not to call attention to ourselves.

"What not to wear" seems provincial now, and most seminaries no longer give clothing advice. Indeed, many ministers, men and women, wear colorful clothing, footwear, hair, and tattoos. Definitions of formal and informal dress are changing as fast as our worship styles and settings. Yet a book by young clergywomen published in 2011 suggests that clergy attire and personal appearance, especially for women, continue to receive both kudos and criticisms from church members and even other clergy. Engaging in ministry as gendered persons entails intentional thoughtfulness regarding our public appearance. As you decide how to express yourself authentically before others, you may consider denominational guidelines, the norms and customs of your ministry context, along with your own preferred style. If you and your supervisor can discuss at the outset customs, expectations, and personal preferences, you will have support if—no, *when* someone chooses to make "your style" an issue.

*[T]here came out from the camp of the Philistines a champion named Goliath,
of Gath, whose height was six cubits and a span. He had a helmet of bronze on
his head, and was armed with a coat of mail; the weight of the coat was five
thousand shekels of bronze. . . . Saul clothed David with his armor; he put a
bronze helmet on his head and clothed him with a coat of mail. David strapped
Saul's sword over the armor, and he tried in vain to walk, for he was not used
to them. . . . So David removed them.* (1 Sam. 17:4–5, 38–39)

We can choose what we wear, but not other things about ourselves. Goliath and David each put on the same clothing, but it didn't fit them the same way! David chose to be himself, using his smaller stature and youthfulness wisely and effectively. Goliath's impressive size did not turn out to be the asset he and everyone else assumed. We may be well over six feet tall or barely five feet high. We may have a voice that thunders across the valley from pulpit to pews or a voice that travels gently on the wings of the Spirit. Physical and vocal differences are not always related to gender, but they can be. A seminary student that I knew of several years ago was six feet eight inches tall and, during internships in a church and later in a hospital setting, had to learn how to use his body more consciously so that others were not overwhelmed by his size. Another student, who was young and very petite, struggled to feel that people took her seriously as an intern. She tired of being treated as someone's daughter or granddaughter and sought her supervisor's advice on how to respond to remarks about her age and small stature. Women in ministry, like women in business and politics, often receive more comments than men regarding their public speaking voices. Men may be granted pastoral authority more freely than women simply because they are males. The internship provides a learning environment for "finding your voice" as a ministerial leader and discovering how to use your voice most effectively in worship, pastoral care settings, and even committee meetings. An internship also offers space to practice "embodying" ministerial leadership in those same arenas. With growing self-awareness and confidence, you will engage gender intentionally as you interact with others. When meeting with someone in your office, do you close the door or leave it open? When do you shake hands or choose to embrace? How do you maintain your preferred physical boundaries and respect those of others as well?

*"I commend to you our sister Phoebe, a deacon of the church. . . . Greet
Prisca and Aquila, who work with me in Christ Jesus. . . . Greet my beloved
Epaenetus. . . . Greet Andronicus and Junia"* (Rom. 16:1–7ff.).

Paul sends greetings to a host of men and women who were leaders and coworkers in ministry. Each no doubt had his or her own style and personality in leading others for the sake of the Gospel. Leadership styles are not limited to gender norms and expectations. On the contrary, responsibilities of ministerial leadership cross, even *overturn*, gender stereotypes. Men in ministry are often in nurturing roles, comfortable with a wide array of emotions. Women in ministry are often powerful leaders, tackling hard decisions, dismantling systems of conflict. In 1995 Sally Purvis studied two clergywomen serving two congregations in the same city. She expected that "gender" was something that "would hold still for us while we looked at other issues." Instead, she found that gender expectations are much more variable, so that two clergywomen, serving two similar congregations only miles apart, could experience their gender quite differently. Purvis observed that "gender as a set of cultural expectations is also always a negotiation, a dynamic, relational reality, so that individual characteristics of every woman will interact in somewhat different ways with social expectations, thereby reinscribing or reinterpreting them in very complex ways."[6] As you observe your supervisor's leadership style and other leadership styles in your ministry setting, you will also be exercising your own emerging style of leading, negotiated within a dynamic relationship with others. I have a friend who is a clergyman. It has taken some time for his congregation to adapt to his leadership style, which is more collaborative than hierarchical. He is less likely to direct new ministry initiatives, preferring instead to let initiatives emerge from within the congregation. The former pastor, a female, preferred a hierarchical, directive leadership approach. Some women planting new churches today believe their cultural upbringing as females (in which collaboration and listening skills were valued) causes them to plant churches differently than their male colleagues do.[7]

"There is no longer Jew or Greek, there is no longer slave or free, there is no longer male and female; for all of you are one in Christ Jesus" (Gal. 3:28).

Meanwhile, here at the church of "We Aren't There Yet," my colleague, Professor of Preaching Anna Carter Florence, has said, "I am waiting for the day when my students will see themselves—and their peers!—as preachers first, rather than *women* preachers and *men* preachers. Because that will be the day we can get on to the business of being *human* preachers, whom God created male and female, with all types of bodies and all ranges of voices and all manners of taste in music, dress, shoes, and tattoos. It will save a lot of time."[8] Anna speaks for many of us who negotiate difficult gender barriers, overcome stereotypes, and field comments that become quite personal. Engaging gender in ministry is not easy, but it can be a dynamic gift of the Spirit. As those tightly drawn, often restrictive gender norms and expectations are reinterpreted and overturned, we are invited more fully into God's extravagance.

QUESTIONS FOR REFLECTION

1. How have you been formed and affected by gender norms and expectations?
2. In your field placement, are there areas of ministry in which traditional gender norms and expectations are being maintained? Being overturned?

SUGGESTED READING

Brown, Teresa L. Fry. *Can a Sistah Get a Little Help? Encouragement for Black Women in Ministry*. Cleveland, OH: Pilgrim Press, 2008.

Deasy, Jo Ann. "Father Images and Women Pastors: How Our Implicit Ecclesiologies Function." *Covenant Quarterly* 72, nos. 3–4 (August–November 2014): 143–157.

Kim, Grace Ji-Sun. *Embracing the Other: The Transformative Spirit of Love*. Grand Rapids, MI: Eerdmans, 2015.

Masters, Asley-Anne, and Stacy Smith. *Bless Her Heart: Life as a Young Clergy Woman*. St. Louis, MO: Chalice Press, 2011.

Sentilles, Sarah. *A Church of Her Own: What Happens When a Woman Takes the Pulpit*. Boston: Mariner Books/Houghton Mifflin Harcourt, 2008.

Spong, Martha, ed. *There's a Woman in the Pulpit*. Woodstock, VT: Skylight Paths Publishing, 2015.

Stewart, Eric C. "Masculinity in the New Testament and Early Christianity." *Biblical Theology Bulletin* 46, no. 2 (2016): 91–102.

Swenson, Erin. "A Transgender Pastor's Story: Becoming Myself." *Christian Century* (March 9, 2010): 28–33.

Chapter Nineteen

Engaging Race

Grace Ji-Sun Kim

I have never felt any problem with the color of my skin. I love my color. I have learned that my skin color is beautiful.

I believe that diversity in skin color adds beauty and richness to our world. This is a beautiful understanding, but the rest of the world may not embrace this. Though I have no problem with my "yellow" skin, other people do. This is a type of racism that prevails in our society. There are other varieties of xenophobia, such as discrimination based on language, dress, religion, and country of origin. Even many *paleface* groups from Europe, such as the Irish, the Italians, and the Slavic cultures, have experienced racism in America's history.

You will encounter challenging questions of race and ethnicity in your field education placement. Martin Luther King Jr. often repeated that Sunday morning is the most segregated hour in America. While the number of racially segregated churches is decreasing, about "86 percent of American congregations (containing 80 percent of religious service attendees) remain overwhelmingly white or black or Hispanic or Asian or other minorities."[1] In the last fifty years, a number of churches have merged to create larger, healthier national churches. Now a variety of discrimination is splitting those same denominations, such as the Evangelical Lutheran Church of America and the Presbyterian Church (USA), over lesbian, gay, bisexual, transgender, and gay (LGBTQ) issues.

There are many reasons Sunday morning is the most segregated hour, but it is difficult to deny the role that racism or some other "us versus them" way of thinking plays in this segregation in the church. You need to ask in your ministry context how it is that race and ethnicity play such an important role. It is too simple an answer to say that people like to worship with those who share their ideas and attitudes.

RACISM

Racism is a system that promotes domination of the vulnerable by a privileged group. It separates and dilutes the power of participants in communities. Our society internalizes and institutionalizes racism so that it may be virtually unconscious. Or at the very least, it is hidden, limited to conversations in which people believe they will not be overheard. Racism is woven deeply into a culture from whose inception racial discrimination has been a regulative force for maintaining stability and growth and for maximizing certain cultural values over others. Racism is a manifestation of the deeply held determination to maintain control by the existing dominant group.[2]

Racism is discrimination which builds walls that minorities cannot easily climb. These racial structures set in place against people of color need to be dismantled. Since it is so deeply ingrained, it will take an enormous effort for the dominant society to unlearn its own racist, sexist, and discriminatory social attitudes and behaviors.

Racism is the understanding that people of one race are inferior to another race. (History shows that the tides of racism ebb and flow. Once, Italians, Polish, and Irish immigrants were marginalized by racism. Now those ethnicities have been annealed into the Western European block of Caucasians, allied against African Americans, Hispanics, Japanese, Chinese, Koreans, Vietnamese, Indians, and most of all, now, Muslims and LGBTQ persons, not to mention women in general, which seems to never go away, in spite of generations of progress.)

Racism has often led to a distorted understanding of self. Like a disease, it spreads throughout one's existence and can be undetected, as it presents itself as a guise for how society exists in the Western world.[3] The result, even in the church, is prejudice, discrimination, and antagonism toward another race.

Racism has always been institutionalized. The two most horrific examples are the "separate but equal" doctrine in the southern US states and the internment of thousands of ethnic Japanese during World War II. It is intrinsic to the structures of societies in several ways. Racism promotes domination of the vulnerable by a privileged group in the economic, social, cultural, and intellectual spheres.[4] Racial discrimination is systematic, racially grounded policies and practices designed to make life more challenging for one race while preserving privilege for the dominant group.[5] This is just as true in nonwhite cultures as it is in Anglo-European cultures. Witness the discrimination of Israel against Palestinians, Shiites against Sunnis, and one black African tribe against another.

There are subtle ways that racism is experienced by people of color. People of color are expected to experience gratefulness to white people for whatever we have achieved. For example, if we are invited to a meeting to engage some very important issue, white people make it clear to people of color that we were "especially invited" and should show gratitude for the invitation. That the table is for white folks and thus, if you get a special invite, you should always be grateful to the white community.

Another way racism plays out is when a college student of color gets into an elite school; he or she is believed to have taken a white student's spot. In the same way, when a person of color lands a job, the white community feels that that job was "taken away" from a white person. This plays into the narrative of white privilege. "White privilege" is the outcome of a pervasive presumption of the racial superiority of whiteness.[6] We need to make the privilege visible and dismantle it. Race is not a social category that stands alone. Racial discrimination is a class distinction, a dynamic interaction with gender, sexuality, and class.

A consequence of racism is becoming a marginalized person. The term *marginalized*, unlike *minority*, emphasizes the process of marginalizing and insists that the relative prestige of languages and cultures and the conditions of their contact are constituted in social relations of ruling in both national and international arenas.[7] The marginalized cultures live in a fragile space of uncertainty, domination, and relative powerlessness. Marginalization is a form of domination and deception. Furthermore, racialized identities are not simply imposed; they are often the outcome of resistance and political struggle in which racialized groups play a key and active role. Thus it may be more accurate to speak of a racialized rather than a racial group, since race is a product of racism and not vice versa.[8]

ASIAN AMERICAN EXPERIENCES OF RACISM

Since I am Asian American, I am viewed as an "honorary white." This is a problematic term, as it begins with the false notion that white is best and that we all need to strive to meet white standards. Whiteness becomes the standard, and all people need to attain this status. Asian Americans are ranked higher than other people of color: not white, but almost good enough. Due to this problematic term, whenever Asian Americans experience racism, society tells us that what we experienced wasn't racism, as we are "honorary whites." It is as if Asian Americans should be immune to this.

A young Korean American female pastor complained to her senior minister about her extended experiences of racism within the church. After much encouragement from her friends, she gathered enough courage to share these painful realities with her senior minister.

After she shared her pain and discrimination, the minister looked at her and said, "You didn't experience racism, you are white!"

With that statement, she was dismissed and all her painful experiences were disqualified as racism. It is difficult that racism within the United States is understood mostly in binary terms, "black and white." If you are not black, then your experiences of racism are not real.

Please recognize that all people of color experience racism. We are not in a competition of who suffered/suffers more. We are in a situation in which we need to stand in solidarity so that we can fight racism. The plea for solidarity is especially important for you to embrace in your field education placement. Your experience right now in recognizing racism and coura-geously addressing it is critical to your future leadership.

Reject terms such as "model minority," used to describe Asian Americans. That term was coined in the 1960s to describe the belief that if the other people of color just studied or worked as hard as the Asian Americans, then they could achieve the American dream. It was a myth to pit one group of people against another group. (It also totally disregarded the fact that racism puts barriers in front of minorities to prevent them from achieving that which whites consider their birthright.) It engenders a "divide and conquer" mentality. If only you worked as hard as the others, you too would succeed. We know very well that a "bamboo ceiling" exists. Asian Americans can only reach a certain stage, and then they cannot get any further. We also know that Asian Americans do not all succeed and get into Ivy League schools.

RACISM WITHIN CHURCH AND MINISTRY

Racism is not a small or disappearing problem. We who grew up in the church, attend a church, or serve a church tend to believe that there is no racism in the church. But racism exists within our church and has caused pain, suffering, and heartache for many of its members and leaders. So let's be honest and engage the racism in our churches and places of ministry as openly as possible.

In one incident a stranger came into a church and was looking for the minister. The minister of the church was there. She said, "I am the minister, can I help you?" The man took another look at her and asked the question, "Can I see the minister?" The minister, who is an African American woman, was humiliated because the white man could not see her as a minister, looked past her, and asked the question again.

When I started seminary, I was involved in various churches either through field education or through leading retreats. One time I had gone to a white church to do pulpit supply. When I entered the church, no one expected an Asian American woman to be a guest preacher. Everyone just assumed I was a visitor, and they could not fathom me as a preacher. They gave me strange looks and treated me as an outsider. This is one of many painful experiences people of color have had in the church.

Subtle racism infiltrates our church and ministerial roles. Even unconsciously we can rank people according to the color of their skin, their gender, their age, or their sexual preferences. You and I, as Christian leaders, need to accept the responsibility to combat racism in the church and the world. We need to do this because racism violates the core of the gospel message.

We want people to be accepted regardless of any difference that sets one person apart from another. But they often are not. We show prejudice against newcomers who are not white. We do this when we assume that they are only visitors and will not return. They may in fact be seeking a congregation and would like to be welcomed into the church!

Our churches can work harder to make a difference in fighting racism. Racism is a sin, and it needs to be countered and eliminated from our churches.

STEPS IN FIGHTING RACISM

How do we fight against racism?

First, we must acknowledge that it exists. Acknowledge publicly the dangers of racism and how it poisons lives, communities, and the church. If we are not building each other up, we are tearing one another down. Link arms in solidarity with fellow Christians to fight racism. Join hands with other persons and groups of goodwill to fight racism. It could literally be a matter of life and death.

Second, we must learn to accept and embrace those who are different from us. We in fact are building walls if we are not tearing them down. In your field education placement, make it your goal to accept diversity and welcome, even celebrate, the differences you encounter.

Third, recognize that we cannot do it alone. It becomes the transformative power of the Spirit that builds bridges and connects us to each other. We must allow the Spirit that brings forth love into the world to form relationships with each other. This love is powerful, as it connects people in different ways.

In Korea we have a term for such connection to each other. It is called *jeong*. This is a connected love that overcomes pain, rough relationships, differences, and even hatred. This *jeong* can move us toward transformation. It can help us fight against racism, which is so pervasive in our society and in our churches.

In so many ways, this is what the Spirit does. The Spirit brings connectedness and love between people: *jeong*. The Spirit helps us love each other, embrace each other, and join one with another with this *sticky* love.

QUESTIONS FOR REFLECTION

1. What group was dominant in the context in which you grew up? How did racism manifest itself?
2. Who is currently addressing racism as a Christian that you can learn from?
3. How can this ministry context take a step forward toward embracing the other?

SUGGESTED READING

Cone, James H. *The Cross and the Lynching Tree.* Maryknoll, NY: Orbis Books, 2013.

Jennings, Willie James. *The Christian Imagination: Theology and the Origins of Race.* New Haven, CT: Yale University Press, 2011.

Kim, Grace Ji-Sun. *Embracing the Other: The Transformative Spirit of Love.* Grand Rapids, MI: Eerdmans, 2015.

Kim, Grace Ji-Sun, ed. *Here I Am: Faith Stories of Korean American Clergywomen.* Philadelphia: Judson Press, 2015.

Chapter Twenty

Engaging in a Nonprofit Context

John E. Senior

The world needs ministry leaders who are called to the work of nonprofit organizations! As you discern your calling to this work, I invite you to consider two related challenges that make nonprofit contexts both distinctive and exciting for ministry leaders. The first has to do with what one might call "translation." In secular nonprofit settings, or even at times in faith-based nonprofit settings, you will have to consider how you will function and what kinds of contributions you will make as a ministry leader in a context in which you may not be identified as a minister. In other words, how will you translate your theological training in ways that empower you to make constructive contributions to secular nonprofit organizations and to the secular audiences that support or are served by those organizations? The second challenge has to do with public leadership. Nonprofit leadership is at its heart a form of public leadership. At the same time that nonprofit organizations provide goods and service to advance the common good, they are in effect also making arguments to broader public audiences about why their work matters and why the community should support it. The public leadership aspect itself relies on forms of translation, as nonprofit leaders have to render the complex work they do every day into narratives that broader publics can understand and want to endorse. I want you to understand that for theologically trained leaders, nonprofit work is a kind of liminal space. You likely won't function ministerially in quite the ways that you've been trained to do in seminary. At the same time, nonprofit organizations can benefit profoundly from the leadership that you have been trained to provide.

Let me share an anecdote that illustrates these two challenges. Several years ago one of our now graduates, wanting to explore the possibility of an internship placement for the upcoming year, arranged to meet with a program coordinator at a local secular nonprofit organization. Our school had not worked with this organization before, and because the organization does excellent work in our community, I was excited to establish a relationship. After the student's initial meeting with his potential supervisor-mentor, the student e-mailed me to say that program coordinator was concerned about the use of "ministry language" in our Covenant of Shared Wisdom. This is the document we use to formalize the internship relationship. There was a concern that since the student would be working under the auspices of programs funded by grants from secular sources, his role could not be formally understood in the framework of "ministry leadership." I happily volunteered to have a follow-up conversation with the program coordinator to clarify the purposes and aims of our field education program.

In our phone conversation, I explained that the School of Divinity understands the idea of ministry leadership in a very broad framing, to include any work in which persons empower others to discern and respond to God's call in their lives, even if that work is done in secular settings and in ways that are not explicitly theological. I emphasized that we strive to equip our students with skills, practices, and interpretive frameworks that can help (even secular) nonprofit organizations in their mission to create and share common goods and to tell compelling stories about why they do what they do. I came away from our conversation with the impression that my attempt at clarification was moderately successful. Though the program coordinator understood where I was coming from, she still seemed a little suspicious that our student might be attempting to proselytize clients or otherwise behave inappropriately.

Of course this internship placement could have backfired. Despite our mentor training program and other structures we provide to guide the internship process, there was a possibility that the mentor fundamentally wouldn't "get" why we think a divinity student could both learn a lot from and make meaningful contributions to a secular nonprofit organization. It's possible that the student would not have a good experience. But I thought that if we were clear and honest about what we were trying to do in the internship placement and also attentive to the student's experience along the way, it would be worth the risk. If we only worked with nonprofit organizations that really understand what theological education is all about, the list would be very short indeed. And I firmly believe that theologically trained leaders have much to contribute to secular and faith-based nonprofit organizations that are making contributions to the flourishing of human communities and of all creation. I believe they can be effective at making arguments in public spaces to public audiences about why their work matters. So I was happy for this internship placement to be a form of persuasion and education about why a secular nonprofit should want a divinity intern, even as it is an educational opportunity for our student.

This anecdote illustrates the kind of conversations I have had with students interested in nonprofit work. It's often not clear, particularly in secular nonprofit organizations, what contributions a theologically trained leader might make to the work of these organizations. Even in faith-based nonprofit organizations, leaders have to learn how to translate their theological commitments into claims accessible to broader public audiences. They are continually making the case for why the communities that nonprofit organizations serve should care about and how they might contribute to the work. On the broadest level they are helping a community understand what it means to be a community. More perhaps than their colleagues trained in law, business, medicine, and other fields of professional education, theologically trained leaders learn moral languages of community building, common goods, and human flourishing. The challenge is to learn how to deploy these moral languages in organizations that may not rely on theological frameworks and to do so faithfully. Another way to say this is that nonprofit organizations need leaders who know how to make meaning of the human longing for justice. Theologically trained leaders are well positioned to do that work, with or without explicit God-talk.

Indeed, meaning making is central to the work of nonprofit organizations. Through their mission and vision statements, good nonprofits clearly identify their vision of the world as it should be and articulate how their work contributes to the fashioning of such a world. Wise nonprofit leaders continually reference their vision and mission statements. They design organizational structures, programs, fund-raising efforts, financial plans, and assessment procedures with a view to achieving the goals that their mission and vision statements lay out.

It is vitally important, then, that you understand the organization's vision and mission. Learn the history and context of that vision, then ask critically whether, how, and to what extent the many aspects of the organization's structure and work contribute to achieving its mission and vision.[1] It is certainly not uncommon that nonprofits stray from their mission and vision, especially when they are attracted to funding opportunities that support work exceeding the purview of the organization's purpose.

My encouragement to you is similar in some ways to the encouragement I would offer to congregational interns. Just as you would in a congregational setting, you should first attend carefully to the local context of the organization's work (see chapter 4, "Engaging Your Context for Ministry"). Consider carefully, with the help of your supervisor-mentor, the cultural, socioeconomic, and historical factors creating the demands for justice to which your nonprofit organization is responding. You should also pay attention to the local nonprofit ecology to understand how the work of your organization fits into the complex web of efforts made by similar organizations responding to similar issues in a local community.

Another of our alumni won a sizable grant to develop a mobile food pantry that provides healthy food to neighborhoods located in food deserts in our city. This former student learned that the largest food provision organizations in town supply their network partners (e.g., church food pantries) with low-cost food. But these larger organizations place restrictions on how often clients can receive food provisions from their network partners and also require identification from clients, effectively discouraging undocumented communities from seeking their services. She has opted, for the time being at least, not to become a network partner so that her mobile food pantry can serve persons and communities excluded by the policies of these larger food provision organizations. That's a good example of how careful analysis of a local nonprofit ecology shapes the aims and purposes of an organization. Be contextually attuned, just as you would if you were serving a congregation.

And just as in congregational settings, you will need to invest time and energy, particularly at the beginning of an internship experience, in building relationships with clients/guests, staff, administrators, and board members of their organization, as well as (ideally) with external community leaders whose work intersects with the work of the internship setting. Following many community organizing models, you will want to build intentional and public relationships with these stakeholders.[2] In one-on-one relational meetings, you should work to

1. identify the stories, values, and energies that disclose a stakeholder's passion for the work of the organization;
2. better understand the aspects of the organization's work that stakeholders are willing to work on—what, as one community organizer puts it, a person will "get off his or her butt for," and why;
3. appreciate the history and culture of the organization;
4. consider the directions in which a stakeholder thinks the organization is moving and/or should be moving;
5. identify where there are productive intersections of interests, such as the interests of the intern and of various stakeholders in the organization; and
6. in light of these conversations, identify what immediate possibilities there are for collaboration. In what ways can an emerging collaboration be held to standards of accountability that document effectiveness and bolster confidence in the collaboration?

Relationships built intentionally around these themes are public in the sense that they focus on what people can achieve together to move the work of the organization forward, and they create accountability structures that push the relationship in the direction of goal-driven collaboration.

Another reality facing leaders in both congregational and nonprofit settings is that ever-expanding demands outstrip the resources of time, energy, money, creativity, and material. Good nonprofit leaders are scrappy in their ability to identify and mobilize resources available for doing the work of their organizations. They are also careful to ensure that their organization is focused on the work prescribed by their mission and vision statements and realistic about the limits of their organization's capacity to do that work, lest the organization drift too far afield or without intending it contribute to staff and leadership burnout. It would be valuable for you to observe the patterns and practices your supervisor-mentor and other organizational leaders have developed to address the challenges of working amid these conditions.

Finally, as you begin to work with your organization's programs and learn about the administration of your organization, it pays to get in the habit of backward design thinking. Try thinking backward from the concrete goals that your organization seeks to accomplish, to considering what kind of process would be needed to produce the desired results, how that process would be assessed for effectiveness, how it would align with the organization's mission and vision, and how the organization would narrate its efforts in ways that would invite broader public audiences to share in and support the mission of the organization.[3] Retrospective thinking from the vantage point of the goals your organization seeks to achieve holds the organization accountable to concrete and measurable outcomes and creates opportunities to check the organization's process and outcomes against its mission and vision.

In many ways, theological education is still wrestling with how ministry leaders can be trained faithfully and effectively to work in nonprofit organizations. I look forward to your learning in this internship process and to hearing your emerging wisdom about what it means to do the work of ministry in these settings.

QUESTIONS FOR REFLECTION

1. Given the challenge of "translation" described above, how do you think about doing the work of nonprofit leadership faithfully as a ministry leader?
2. What draws you to the work of nonprofit leadership? What gifts do you bring to that work? And how do you think your theological education can prepare you to do that work well?

SUGGESTED READING

Block, Peter. *Community: The Structure of Belonging*. Oakland, CA: Berrett-Koehler Publishers, 2009.

Essau, Jill, and Stanley W. Carlson-Thies. *Start and Grow Your Faith-Based Nonprofit: Answering Your Call in the Service of Others*. San Francisco: Jossey-Bass, 2005.

Heyman, Darian Rodriguez. *Nonprofit Management 101: A Complete and Practical Guide for Leaders and Professionals*. San Francisco: Jossey-Bass, 2011.

Chapter Twenty-One

Engaging in Clinical Pastoral Education

Jim Rawlings, Jr.

Whether you have decided to enroll in a program of clinical pastoral education (CPE), or your field education director or judicatory body has encouraged this, you are about to enter a transformative experience.[1] You will be invited to engage in ministry (action), reflect upon that experience (reflection), and then, learning from this interaction, engage in another pastoral encounter (the action). This process is called the clinical method of learning, and it lies at the heart of the CPE process. It serves to develop awareness of self, understanding of ministry, and interpersonal skills.

THE CLINICAL PASTORAL EDUCATION PROCESS

The CPE process occurs both individually and communally. Individually, you will meet on a regular basis with your CPE supervisor.[2] As you begin this process, your supervisor will ask you what you want to learn from your participation in the program. This question may seem odd to you. Yet the very open-endedness of the query creates the opportunity to engage in reflection on what is currently significant to you. Your supervisor will help you identify goals that are relevant to you, as well as attainable during the time you will be involved in the program. Throughout your CPE training, you will meet regularly with your supervisor to review your learning goals, pastoral encounters, participation in and with your peer group, and relationship with your supervisor. At the conclusion of the program, you will write a final evaluation and share it with your peer group. You will be provided a final evaluation of your work by your supervisor with an opportunity to discuss your CPE experience.

Communally, you will be part of a group of fellow students. Groups typically are made up of three to six members. The CPE curriculum will involve time for each member to share his or her pastoral care conversations, called verbatim;[3] reflections on assigned readings in a seminar style method, didactics;[4] and group processing of what is personally and professionally relevant for him or her.

The largest portion of your time in the CPE process will be your engagement with the "living human document."[5] Today, CPE is offered primarily in accredited centers located within acute care hospitals.[6] In these centers you will be assigned a patient unit(s). Your role will be that of the chaplain.[7] In these hospital units, you will encounter individuals whose lives have been altered by illness or injury. These persons will look to you as pastor, the one who comes to them with good news to assuage their anguish. On such occasions you will begin to question what you have to offer them. Or patients will look at you and see all that is wrong with their lives, and their anger at God may be expressed as "go away, I don't need you or God." Most difficult for me is the person who does not even acknowledge me and remains silent. You will struggle with the rationale for ministry in such a place. These experiences will challenge your calling to be a pastor and provide you with experiences upon which to reflect with yourself, in your peer group, and with your supervisor.

Hospital staff also are part of your "parish." As a chaplain-intern,[8] you will observe the busyness of staff as they move from one task to another and seemingly are indifferent to you. In your parish field education experience, you probably found yourself more comfortable with the parishioners' expectations, and your role was familiar. In the hospital setting many persons will not understand your role. They may wonder why your presence is necessary. This experience is uncomfortable. It may challenge you to clarify further your call to ministry. In the parish setting the pastor historically has been held in high esteem. His or her role carries a certain authority. In the hospital setting the authority is the physician. What does this different status mean for you? Has your authority somehow been diminished by the physician's presence? The setting can at times feel like a place of "dry bones."[9] How do you engage such an experience? What do you understand about your calling? Yourself? Your ability to care for another? Your competence as a pastor? How have you been formed—educationally, theologically, culturally, and experientially—to address these situations?

To engage these questions and thoughts is difficult. No one-two-three-step plan will, in the end, be satisfactory for you. You might seek out the familiarity of family, friends, and God to find reassurance that you are called to be a pastor. And these resources will provide the necessary comfort. Yet the critical issue is whether or not you are willing to engage the action-reflection-action process to earnestly move into your uncomfortableness, or more aptly put, the "valley of the shadows";[10] having faith, you will learn more about yourself, your competencies, and your style of ministry.

HOW YOU MIGHT BEST ENGAGE IN CPE

Up to this point I have described the process of CPE. Here's how you might engage this process for its marvelous potential for learning. I like the acronym H-O-W[11] to think about engaging CPE. H stands for *honesty*. In CPE, I think about how honest persons can be with themselves, another person, and God. To be honest with oneself is really quite risky. Our human tendency is to deny our weaknesses and focus on our strengths. When asked, students are often amazed that it has been those experiences of struggle that have afforded them the greatest learning.

You will have ample opportunities to be honest or not. I encourage you to take the risk and be honest: honest with yourself when you do not know what to do or say and to ask for guidance. One of the beautiful aspects of CPE is that you can ask and you have a person to ask: your supervisor. Also, be honest with the other persons when asked a question you do not have an answer to.

During my first on-call experience I was paged, early in the morning, to the room of a young mother. She had been admitted to the hospital with smoke inhalation. I conferred with the nurse, who shared with me the following. The woman's husband, prior to leaving home for the third shift at the local factory, had filled their wood-burning stove with wood to keep her and the children warm during the night. Sometime around midnight, the eight-year-old son awoke and smelled smoke. He rushed into his mother's room and helped her out of their single-wide trailer. After securing her safety, he returned to the trailer to rescue his six-year-old sister. Overcome by smoke, the young boy and his sister died. When I entered the mother's room that Saturday morning, she was sitting up in bed, watching cartoons on television. And she was laughing. I could not even go in the room, as my anger flared. "How could she be so callous? Her children were dead, she was alive and watching cartoons."

I reflected on this experience for several days prior to having individual supervision with my supervisor. I remember sitting down in one of the chairs in his office and exclaiming my disbelief at this woman's behavior. He looked at me and asked, "How do you understand her behavior, given what she has been through?" This was my first encounter with attempting to understand what a person might experience after experiencing severe trauma. This experience impacted me deeply. Attempting to look through another's eyes was a new concept for me. Had I not brought my experience to supervision and processed that experience, I might never have known just how judgmental or how insensitive to another's pain I could be. This young mother had lost two of her children, and to cope, for the moment, she found a cartoon to ease her intense suffering. I did not engage ministry that day with that mother, but my actions became instructive. Through reflection, I learned much about myself and how we, as human creatures, react and respond to trauma. I invite you to bring your honesty to the CPE process, where the potential for learning always exists.

Openness is a word expressing willingness to be as transparent as one can. Transparency expresses a level of humility and vulnerability in which the individual's internal and external senses are congruent, allowing that person to be who he or she is with little pretense. I believe this is part of what it means to be in a right relationship with one's self, others, and God. In the CPE process, openness helps to create a safe space for individuals to engage one another and enhance the possibility of learning from each other.

For a good part of my ministerial career I worked hard to prove to others that I was a competent person, husband, father, pastor, and chaplain. There were few challenges I did not engage in an effort to prove my worthiness. When a peer in my CPE group confronted me about this behavior, I immediately became defensive, claiming that I did just the opposite. I was not being open to his feedback and even denied his words. My behavior was not congruent with how I understood the Gospel. I was not being honest and open with him, my family, friends, colleagues, and God about my fears and anxieties. When the time came for me to be open, I was scared. After all, if these people really knew how inadequate I felt, they would drum me out of ministry. It took several confrontations before I found the courage to be open about my deep sense of insecurity. Rather than being ridiculed, I was embraced. One colleague said, "Do you think you are any different than any of the biblical characters you have read about or people since?" In that moment, I felt grace. A gift that had been available all along, but I had been unwilling to open myself to the experience.

I invite you to come into the CPE process with as much openness as possible. Open to learning from each experience you have. Open to hearing the small but powerful voices within you. Open to hearing what others have to say to you. And open to yourself and open to God.

The final leg of this three-pronged acronym is *willingness*. To engage the CPE process requires one to be willing to learn, willing to risk, and willing to grow as a person and a pastor. Are you willing to learn from not only the supervisor but also your peers and the patients with whom you will minister? To bring this attitude into the CPE process will create, for you, the opportunity for many life lessons, lessons you will carry with you throughout your ministry.

During a yearlong residency[12] I was paged to the room of a young man, my age at the time, who was experiencing rejection of a transplanted kidney.

He had called for a chaplain to visit. I was on call that day and responded. Entering the room, I seated myself next to him and asked how he was doing. All he could do was moan and cry out from his pain. Every part of me wanted to say a prayer and leave. For some reason, I did not leave. For the next several hours, I sat beside him holding his hand and occasionally wiping his forehead with a cool washcloth. I have reflected on this experience many times. Upon reflection, I realized I had no words, no wisdom, and no theological acumen to offer this young man, who was dying. What I did have was a willingness to sit with him for a while in that dark, shadowy space of life. Possibly I lessened his sense of loneliness and fear. He never spoke a word to me, but his cries of pain ebbed and he was able to sleep, at least for awhile. I invite you, no matter how tired, resistant, anxious, or hurried you might feel, to remind yourself to remain willing to step into these shadowy places with folks and allow God to speak to and through you whether or not words are uttered.

In this brief description of how you might engage in CPE, I've offered you some of my thoughts and experiences in the hope they will be helpful as you anticipate enrolling in ACPE-CPE. As one student wrote at the end of her CPE experience, "This has been the most difficult and rewarding experience of my seminary career. I have grown as a person and a pastor into a more confident individual. I now know I do not have answers to the most difficult of life's questions, but I do know that when confronted with a situation, I am not alone and that I do have something to offer the other person. That offering is not 'silver or gold,'[13] but myself, my faith, and my hope." And this is sufficient.

QUESTIONS FOR REFLECTION

1. What do you hope to learn about yourself, ministry, and God by serving in a clinical setting?
2. Recall a time when you grew in self-awareness and personal maturity through a challenging experience. How do you carry that learning in your person today?

SUGGESTED READING

Clinebell, Howard. *Basic Types of Pastoral Care and Counseling: Resources for the Ministry of Healing and Growth*. Nashville, TN: Abingdon, 2011.
Doehring, Carrie. *The Practice of Pastoral Care: A Postmodern Approach*. Westminster, KY: John Knox Press, 2015.
Gerkin, Charles V. *The Living Human Document*. Nashville, TN: Abingdon, 1984.
Hall, Charles E. *Head and Heart: The Story of the Clinical Pastoral Education Movement*. Decatur, GA: Journal of Pastoral Care Publications, 1992.

Holst, Lawrence. *Hospital Ministry: The Role of the Chaplain Today*. Eugene, OR: Wipf & Stock, 2007.
Nouwen, Henri J. M. *The Wounded Healer*. New York: Image Books, 1979.
Taylor, Barbara Brown. *Learning to Walk in the Dark*. New York: Harper One, 2014.

Chapter Twenty-Two

Engaging Technology in Field Education

Susan E. Fox

Are you familiar with the syndicated newspaper cartoon "The Pluggers?" It features salt-of-the-earth characters who use their commonsense, plaid-shirt wisdom to adapt to the modern world. As a member of the baby boom generation, technology crept in on me when I was in my thirties. Common use of the Internet was still years in the future, but in true Plugger fashion, I embraced the present and purchased a basic word processor to take with me to seminary in 1985. This amazing machine made typewriter correction tape obsolete! With a simple backspace, typing errors could be erased. I didn't care about anything else the computer could do—which, in reality, was very little. When I arrived at seminary, a friendly second-year student offered to help me unpack my car. She reached for the computer, disguised in its hard plastic case, and said, with some confusion, "Oh . . . you brought your sewing machine!"

Well into the twenty-first century, technology is so pervasive that for some, observing a Sabbath includes going off the grid. Chances are that you don't remember a world without the Internet, and life without Facebook is a distant memory. Indeed, the use and understanding of social networking, digital content, and mobile computing are essential skills for ministry today.

Let me be clear about my starting point on the subject of technology: it is a means to an end that, when used appropriately, can enhance our ability to participate in communities of learning and to serve effectively and creatively in our respective internships. While some accuse technology of destroying our ability to connect at a personal level, when we engage technology strategically and ethically, it can actually promote community without requiring proximity. Author Madeleine L'Engle writes, "There is nothing so secular that it cannot be sacred, and that is one of the deepest messages of the Incarnation."[1] I find L'Engle's statement a helpful lens through which to consider technology in theological field education.

In this chapter I share some of the best technology-related practices that I have picked up over the years, many of which I learned from my students. First I consider resources for the academic side of internships, then tools that can greatly enhance your ministry in your congregational or agency setting.

ACADEMICS

If your seminary or divinity school uses a Web-based learning management system (LMS) such as Moodle, Blackboard, Canvas, or Acatar, you have excellent resources at your fingertips. Learning management systems typically provide similar features: class announcements, assignment submission, discussion boards, chat rooms, file uploads, and gradebooks.

Discussion boards are often used when your seminary instructor wants you to reflect on a question or topic with your fellow interns outside of the physical classroom setting. For example, let's assume that your class has been given the assignment to read a case study that describes a difficult pastoral visit to a family that has just experienced the death of an incarcerated parent/spouse. Each of you is to respond to the statement, "Identify and briefly discuss two theological issues present in this situation." Introverts will welcome the fact that discussion boards are asynchronous; that is, you have time to reflect deeply on the question. And unlike an individual assignment that you submit directly to your instructor, on a discussion board you get to learn from reading your peers' responses.

In addition to LMSs, there are Web-based applications that enable interns to interact with each other and with the seminary instructor by phone or video conferencing. Skype, FaceTime, and Google Hangouts are examples of these real-time (synchronous) collaborative applications. Conferencing applications are also available for downloading on tablets, smartphones, or iPhones, making this technology highly mobile. A word to the wise: if you are using a computer or laptop for these bandwidth-guzzling programs, it is best to be connected via a DSL (telephone) or Ethernet (network) connection rather than Wi-Fi. It's very frustrating for everyone on the conference call to have to pause the conversation because someone using Wi-Fi has a bad connection or gets disconnected. One other suggestion: well before the appointed time for the conference call, make sure you have downloaded the latest version of the program *and* that you have at hand any required user-names/passwords/meeting numbers.

Knowing the technology that is available to you is step one. Step two is entirely in your hands: what, when, and how you communicate via the applications. Take seminarian Jake, for example. Jake had a gregarious personality and was an excellent theologian. Engage him in a face-to-face conversation about a social justice issue, and his passion and insights were compelling. When it came to posting on a discussion board, though, Jake's voice was usually late or missing entirely. When he did post, his comments tended to be superficial, and some were tinged with sarcasm. Several of his peers mentioned to me as the instructor that his lackadaisical attitude was disruptive to the group.

There are several things to learn from Jake, the resistant contributor. Clearly Jake's preferred learning style did not include posting on a discussion board. The theory of multiple intelligences tells us that students learn and understand in different ways, so chances are that some assignments are not going to resonate with us as much as others. However, Jake's halfhearted participation impacted not only his grade, but the entire learning community. His sarcasm was occasionally experienced as insensitivity, leading to misunderstanding among his peers. Nuances that he intended to convey simply were not communicated in typed words. Finally, the insights Jake could have brought to the conversation were lost because of his halfhearted contributions. If Jake had made the commitment to approach the discussion board as sacred space, I suspect that he might have responded differently.

ON SITE

Even before you go to your field education placement, you can begin a preliminary contextual analysis of your ministry setting. The more you familiarize yourself with the congregation or agency, the easier it will be for you to navigate the early days of your internship. If your setting has a Web site, begin there. Depending on its level of sophistication, you might find newsletters, a calendar of events, and a welcome page that describes the mission and vision and worship style and provides music, links to sermons, listings of educational programs, the church budget, organizational structure, and board/committee/leadership council members. What theological statement does the site imply? Are children integral to the life of the congregation? What is the congregation's role in the community? Does the Web site list any mission partners in the community?

Understanding the congregational or agency culture extends to its utilization of technology. Whether you are serving a community of sophisticated iPhone users who expect a sight and sound show during worship, or you are in a small congregation that relies on the pastor's lung capacity for audio projection, you will need to learn the spoken and unspoken rules about the use of technology in internal and external communications, worship, education, and administration.

Maria was serving a small congregation in rural North Carolina. As was the practice of this congregation, she had been given a parsonage to use during her internship. The home was equipped with a land-line telephone and answering machine, two items that Maria had last used about ten years before. Maria's supervisor left for a week of vacation, leaving her in charge of pastoral care and the Sunday worship service. About three days into her solo service, she ran into a very angry parishioner in the local grocery store who demanded to know why she had not been by to see Mrs. Murphy in the hospital. Maria was devastated; she had no idea that the eighty-year-old charter member was ill. Upon returning to the parsonage, she noticed the red "message" light blinking on the answering machine. Sure enough, three messages had been left about Mrs. Murphy's hospitalization.

Maria had to make a concerted effort to regain the trust of the congregation. Her mistake was to assume that someone at the church would call her cell phone in the event of an emergency. She had shared her number with the board chair, her site committee, and the part-time volunteer secretary. The default process of calling the parsonage phone proved mightier than the intern's request that her cell phone number be used in case of an emergency.

Congregational/agency patterns of technological usage existed before your arrival, and they likely will exist after your departure. Your job is to ferret out the patterns and engage in them. Respond helpfully but very cautiously if you are asked to "improve" some long-standing process, and seek the wisdom of your supervisor-mentor and site team before you lead the charge into the twenty-first century with a new implementation of technology.

LESSONS LEARNED THE HARD WAY

Many of my greatest learnings stem from personal experience—mine or someone else's. Here are some of my favorites:

1. When writing a text, tweet, e-mail, or blog post, imagine the recipient(s) standing over your shoulder reading your words. Even better, visualize the congregational matriarch's or board chairperson's reaction to your words. Revise them if you have the slightest twinge of apprehension about how they will be received.
2. Test the audiovisual equipment before you intend to use it in a presentation or worship service. Does it work? Is it compatible with your computer? Is the Wi-Fi signal strong enough—assuming it exists? My phone carrier's Wi-Fi "hotspot" has bailed me out of a tight spot more than once!

3. Be prepared for audiovisual equipment to fail, despite your efforts to follow the advice in number 2 above. If you plan to use a slide show, print handout copies of the slides to share as a backup. Going to share a movie clip? Be ready to share a synopsis of the scene with the group or have an alternate activity prepared.

4. Bring your adapters (e.g., micro to USB) and extension cords everywhere you plan to use your computer. As a Mac user, I've learned that most institutions still use PCs and that I'd better come prepared with every cord and adapter in my arsenal.

5. Ask your supervisor-mentor and site-team chairperson his or her preferred method of communication—then use it.

6. Know when to turn your phone off. A very agitated site supervisor recently contacted me to report an embarrassing—not to mention highly inappropriate—situation that had occurred during a pastoral care visit. This well-meaning supervisor had brought the intern along to visit a family that had just experienced the death of a loved one. In the midst of discussing plans for the memorial service, the intern pulled out her phone and began sending text messages. Clearly this is an egregious example of poor cell phone *and* pastoral etiquette, but a basic rule of thumb is to silence your phone any time you are called to be present with a parishioner or client. Set your phone to "vibrate" if you are expecting an emergency call and explain to the person or group you are with that you may need to take a call.

7. Use your smartphone to keep yourself organized. Make friends with Siri, her Windows cousin, Cortana, or Android-based Google Now. During your internship, these personal assistant applications can remind you of your existing appointments, set new appointments, set reminders (e.g., "ask Janet about borrowing her commentary before I leave the office"), get directions, set an alarm, and more.

8. Know and abide by your congregation's or agency's social media policy. If there is not one, this may be the time to ignore my advice about bringing the institution into the twenty-first century. Politely suggest that it might be wise to develop a policy!

9. On the subject of social media, Facebook usage deserves special attention. Talk with your supervisor-mentor about institutional policies that exist. If there is no policy, use sound judgment about "friending" members—especially youth. Some youth pastors won't friend a youth member without first getting the approval of a parent or guardian. Now is a good time to take a look at your Facebook account. What is visible to the public? Are there some photos that might be best relegated to close friends only? Remember that your Facebook account reflects on you, the seminary, and your setting.

10. Understand the privacy policies of your church or agency. What types of information can be shared publicly? Is it appropriate to post prayer concerns on the congregation's Web site or Facebook page?

Whether you are a Plugger or a tech geek, you will enter a field education setting whose culture is located somewhere along the technological spectrum of dial-up modem to fiber optics. Even within a single congregation or agency, there will be tremendous technological diversity and a lack of unanimity regarding the "sacred" potential of postmodern communication. When navigating technology in your internship, a healthy dose of wisdom, active listening, and patience and a great sense of humor are tools that will seldom let you down!

QUESTIONS FOR REFLECTION

1. What is your greatest challenge in using technology in academic coursework?
2. To what degree do the constituents of your internship setting embrace technology?
3. What are some technological resources that you and the constituents of your internship setting might utilize well? Where might there be differences in technological openness/ability between you and the constituents of your setting?

SUGGESTED READING

Anderson, Keith. *The Digital Cathedral: Networked Ministry in a Wireless World*. Harrisburg, PA: Morehouse Publishing, 2015.
Drescher, Elizabeth, and Keith Anderson. *Click 2 Save: The Digital Ministry Bible*. Harrisburg, PA: Morehouse Publishing, 2012.
Gould, Meredith. *The Social Media Gospel: Sharing the Good News in New Ways*. Collegeville, MN: Liturgical Press, 2013.
United Methodist Communications. "Connecting with the "Plugged-in" at Your Church—United Methodist Communications." http://www.umcom.org/learn/connecting-with-the-plugged-in-at-your-church (accessed June 1, 2016).
Wise, Justin. *The Social Church: A Theology of Digital Communication*. Chicago: Moody Publishers, 2014.

Chapter Twenty-Three

Engaging Ministry in Secular Settings

Laura S. Tuach

With the religious landscape in North America rapidly changing, ministry is challenged to change and innovate to meet the needs of people outside of traditional religious communities. Ministry happens in all places, whether in a congregational or health-care setting, a grassroots organization or public school. If you choose to work in a secular space for your field education placement, the work you do will be ministry. It is your task to explore how this is so and what ministry means to you in this setting. You will, if you respectfully listen to the context and the people you engage. Explore this in conversation with your supervisor-mentor, colleagues, and possibly the people you serve. Pay attention to how others are making meaning and draw upon your studies, spiritual practices, and experiences to further your discernment process. Ask yourself questions: How is this work ministry for me? How will I explore ministry in a way that supports my educational and vocational goals?

In this chapter you will find a guide to engaging ministry in secular settings. I use a specific case to illuminate some of the questions raised by those exploring settings that are not explicitly religious. I also offer some practical tips to get the most out of your experience.

Jessie is a second-year master of divinity student engaged in field education at a local social services agency whose mission is to provide educational and socioeconomic development services to the refugee and immigrant communities. Jessie sees herself as a "None."[1] She currently identifies as a humanist with a Christian upbringing. In addition to her studies, she is engaged in a community of like-minded people who gather weekly for study sessions on ethical living and centering meditation practices. Jessie is eager to work with her supervisor-mentor, who oversees the case managers in the agency. Her supervisor-mentor shared with her during the interview that she is a lifelong Christian and active in a local congregation that serves immigrant families from Africa. Jessie will be learning from the case managers and will eventually have several cases of her own as the central component of her internship. She is excited to draw upon her volunteer experience in nonprofits before her return to graduate school. As Jessie prepares to begin her placement, she considers what her role will be and how her ethical worldview will be received.

ENGAGE THE CONTEXT RESPECTFULLY

In *Humble Inquiry*, Edward Schein teaches leaders the art of asking and not telling. He argues that too often in Western culture managers lead by telling their teams what to do rather than listening to them with curiosity and humility. When we tell more than we ask, we miss how others orient to the challenges they face. We miss how they are making meaning and in turn miss opportunities to minister with humility. Schein uses the concept "here and now humility," which acknowledges that the person with more knowledge and power is dependent upon those in subordinate roles. People in higher positions can learn more when they approach by listening with the genuine belief that they do not have all the answers or know the best way forward in solving complex problems. Students know all too well that they are in roles in which they depend upon others for learning. Schein argues that supervisor-mentors also depend on students for learning. Likewise, Jessie is dependent on her clients for key learning. They will teach her how to be a minister in this context.

You, too, can take cues from Schein's thesis in your new context. Be curious about what you observe. Do more listening than telling. Engage in humble inquiry by using phrases like "Tell me more about that"; "What else happened?"; and "What do you think should happen next?"[2] Jessie may use these questions when working with refugee families to learn more about their history and what services they need. The more you listen, the more you will be drawing conclusions from what you hear rather than what you infer. You will maximize your learning by listening and asking open-ended questions with "here and now humility."[3]

This approach will also help you to understand the context you are in. You may want to experiment using different open-ended questions as you learn the culture of the organization. Too often we enter new situations trying to prove how competent we are. For example, Jessie brings a lot of nonprofit experience to her field education placement. After a few short days on the job, she has ideas about improving the organization's programs. Does she have enough information yet to be giving suggestions? Has she built enough trust in her relationships with coworkers to offer this critique? Without listening deeply to this new context, she may miss out on critical learning and hinder the relationship-building process.

As a humanist, Jessie may feel compelled to share her belief that humans have all they need in each other and don't need a concept of God to help them through difficult times. In doing so she not only may offend the clients, but also may dismiss a client's desire to talk about God's blessings in the midst of the chaos of resettling. She may miss where their strength comes from and where their grief lies. She may move ahead too quickly and make decisions without considering the fullness of their religious ideals and most basic needs. Most important, Jessie may miss an opportunity to build trust with the families she serves and to minister in the way they most need. In ministry, we learn how to listen so that others feel safe to surface their beliefs, values, and needs. I encourage you to slow down and listen, rather than prematurely rush to "telling" or to judgment and conclusions.[4] Through humble inquiry, acknowledge and depend on the people you serve to guide your next steps in your placement.

When you are engaged in theological studies while working in a secular context, listen to how religious commitments are or are not shared. In this setting Jessie hears the clients openly sharing their belief in God, but religious language is rarely used by the people she works with. She notices that her supervisor shares a little about her faith with Jessie privately. Jessie will engage in personal reflection and reflection about the environment she works in. Jessie will ask herself: Why do I bristle when they talk about God in this way? How do I engage them when I disagree with this concept of God? While reflecting on the organization she will ask: Why are faith commitments openly shared by clients and unspoken by staff? Will she share her belief system with clients and coworkers other than her supervisor-mentor?

In some contexts you may meet people who are confused about your studies. You may even be greeted with suspicion or cynicism. As you engage the context respectfully, pay attention to how you are received when people hear you are exploring ministry. Are jokes made about belief or religious leaders? Or are you received with curiosity? In a secular setting you will be an interpreter of the broad definition of ministry and how you are exploring your beliefs and deepest-held values in the work you engage. For example, Jessie may share her commitment to ethical decision making that is based on a belief in the importance of including all voices in a given community. She doesn't need to mention her spiritual practices or her emerging humanist identity. Through her interactions she will express her belief in the dignity and worth of all human beings. I encourage you to take your cues from the context about how to talk about your studies and preparation for ministry.

If it becomes clear that you should only use explicitly religious language with your supervisor, this does not mean you cannot make meaning with your colleagues about your shared work. As you listen, pay attention to what is important to them. Ask yourself: What are they passionate about? What do they most value about the organization? Does it help them fulfill a sense of meaning or purpose in their lives? Learn from them how they understand the contributions they are making to the mission of the organization. Some may openly talk about their own faith convictions out of a particular tradition. Others may reveal their worldview in other ways. Notice how the organization does or does not welcome these kinds of conversations. In secular settings it is quite common that the pace and volume of the work simply don't allow for this kind of reflective work. I encourage you to reflect on how meaning is made at an individual and organizational level.

ENGAGING THEOLOGICAL REFLECTION WITH YOUR SUPERVISOR

Just as you will educate the people you work with about ministry and your course of study, you will also do this with your supervisor-mentor. She or he may have a faith orientation, but not necessarily have training in theological studies. Therefore it is your responsibility to share program expectations and the reasons you consider this kind of work ministry. I encourage you to discuss how you will engage theological supervision by starting with your definition of *theological*. Some people define theological reflection as addressing the question: How is God present in this situation? For others it is exploring ultimate concern, or the beauty in nature, or being moved by music or poetry. I encourage you to find a way to talk about your worldview, whether through a faith tradition or otherwise. As you make meaning in your supervisory sessions, what resources will you draw from to give language to your emerging theology? To make meaning, will you look to your faith tradition, your values, or your experiences in various body-centered spiritual practices, such as yoga or tai chi? As Jennifer Ayers argues in *Waiting for a Glacier to Move: Practicing Social Witness*, "Theological reflection must be adaptable for a variety of contexts." Her work with activists confronts their anxiety that theological reflection could be mistaken for form of proselytizing.[5] When in secular settings you may experience this fear or, as described previously, others may fear this when they learn you are engaged in ministry. How will you reflect on these experiences? What will you learn about how to phrase things for the widest audience to understand?

I also encourage you to discuss with your supervisor-mentor the best way to prepare for your supervisory sessions. At the beginning of the placement identify particular theological, organizational, and professional questions you have. Describe how you are relating the questions to your sense of call, ministerial identity, and relationship to authority. Work with your supervisor-mentor so that you can explore your understanding of leadership and your needs for professional development. Once you have framed your supervisory sessions, make the most of your weekly reflection time by arriving with prepared thoughts on a specific topic.

PRACTICAL TIPS FOR THEOLOGICAL REFLECTION SESSIONS

You may want to begin your placement by reading a shared text or article that gives you and your supervisor-mentor common ground to discuss. For example, Jessie wants to explore grief in her work with refugees. She may select a book that shares a theoretical look at grief[6] or seek out scriptural passages from various religious traditions that illuminate the experiences of strangers in a strange land.[7] Her supervisor may suggest she read the organization's newsletter articles that highlight the stories of their clients. Beginning with a common text gives focus to those first sessions and often helps you begin to build a relationship of trust with one another.

Perhaps you will write a one-page reflection each week and send it to your supervisor-mentor within a day or two of your meeting. This will allow her to see your thinking about an issue, while giving her the time to think about the topic as well. In a secular setting, how will you choose what you write about? In this written reflection you may want to identify an encounter, incident, or process you observed that you would like to engage in deeper reflection. What questions arise for you? What aspects of the experience are you confused or angered or saddened by? What does this tell you about your values and deeply held beliefs? How might you draw from your courses or faith tradition to shed more light on your own worldview/emerging theology?

Share your academic interests and work with your supervisor-mentor. Are there particular academic topics that are burning for you? Are you proud of certain projects or papers you recently submitted? You may spend some time sharing these ideas and work with her and other colleagues. Field education is a place to integrate your studies and academic goals with your work in the field. Bring your experiences into the classroom with you to see how the theory in both places is operating, coalescing, or not. This integrative work will help you to further explore, discern, and articulate your vision for your ministry. Over time this kind of intentional integration will reveal not only your gifts for ministry but also the places you still need to grow and learn.

As you move through your placement, you will be discerning how this experience is moving you closer to expressing your highest values. Every field education placement is an opportunity to discern your call. Be open to exploring the full range of experiences, even if they make you uncomfortable and disrupt your future plans. While Jessie was convinced at the beginning of her placement that she did not need to be in a setting in which she could openly talk about her ethical commitments and meditation practice, over time she learned that she longed for these kinds of conversations in the workplace. She enjoyed working with the families and being of direct service to them but was surprised that she yearned to be leading healing circles in which people shared their traumas and hopes for a more peaceful world. I encourage you to be open to changes in you as you continue your studies and engage field education. Discernment is ongoing, and every new encounter reveals to us our gifts and passions and offerings in ministry. You will be left with unanswered questions, and your understanding of its meaning will evolve overtime. When you engage in secular settings with intention and the goal of being of service, you will be engaging ministry and serving people where they are instead of waiting for them to come to you.

QUESTIONS FOR REFLECTION

1. How might you articulate that administrative work in an agency setting is ministry?
2. If you are in a field education placement that does not include direct service, what types of things will you reflect on?

SUGGESTED READING

Ayers, Jennifer R. *Waiting for a Glacier to Move: Practicing Social Witness*. Eugene, OR: Pickwick, 2011.
Killen, Patricia O'Connell, and John de Beer. *The Art of Theological Reflection*. New York: Crossroad Publishing, 1999.
Schein, Edgar H. *Humble Inquiry*. San Francisco: Berrett-Koehler Publishers, 2013.

Chapter Twenty-Four

Engaging in an International Field Education

Chester Polk

What is it like to engage in an international field education placement? Try the analogy of a high-wire balancing act. This analogy addresses the essential elements of international field education and directs our attention to the preparatory and precautionary measures necessary to undertake such a challenging—and thrilling—endeavor.

In a high-wire act, skilled performers scale a ladder to the tune of mesmerizing music, ascending high above the circus floor. Their ascent ends atop a platform that leads to the purpose for the journey: the high wire. There is, of course, a net below to catch them in the event that they should fall. Nevertheless, there is no guarantee that they will avoid injury. After a performer has taken a spill, onlookers may assume that he has escaped unscathed. However, occasional scrapes and bruises go unnoticed beneath the dim lights of the big tent. In good form, the performer dismounts the net, throws up his hands to assure the crowd that all is well, then sprints off to scale the ladder yet again. No one may notice that his arm scraped the wire on the way down. After all, mistakes happen. But the show must go on!

The high-wire act is an apt analogy for engaging in international field education, because "balance" is central to both endeavors. In both, physical and mental equilibrium are strained. The performer has much more to be concerned about than constantly making physical adjustments. Therefore many elements of the performance must become second nature to the performer so that he can focus on the other people who are depending on him.

As a student embracing the challenges of an international placement, you must be ever cognizant of the importance of mutual, informative interactions between theoretical and contextual learning—that is to say, of balance. Such interactions set the stage for all that is to follow. Similar interactions—keeping the word "balance" in view—are vital to the student-supervisor relationship, especially if your ministry is to be effective within a context that will be new to you in so many ways.

International site supervisors have emphasized the importance of stimulating students' inquisitive nature regarding their placement and its context before they arrive on site. A ten- to twelve-week placement is a narrow window of opportunity to learn so much, given the circumstances. In order to learn as much as you can and perhaps even form meaningful, lifelong relationships, you must climb up the "ladder" of preparation toward the high wire by acquiring some sense of awareness of the placement country's history, culture, and language. A considerable amount of the learning will include self-awareness, which demands a three-way conversation among you, the supervisor, and God. Yes, there it is again: equilibrium cloaked in theological reflection and a three-dimensional relationship.

In keeping with the high-wire act motif, the platform for such a relationship and effort requires nothing short of a dialogue—not a monologue. Leonard Swidler published an article in the *Journal of Ecumenical Studies* in 1983, "The Dialogue Decalogue: Ground Rules for Interreligious Dialogue," which has been employed effectively in other applications well beyond interreligious work. Swidler's "first commandment" provides sage advice:

> The primary purpose of dialogue is to change and grow in the perception and understanding of reality and then to act accordingly. Minimally, the very fact that I learn that my dialogue partner believes "this" rather than "that" proportionally changes my attitude toward her; and a change in my attitude is a significant change in me. We enter into dialogue so that we can learn, change, and grow, not so we can force change on the other, as one hopes to do in debate—a hope which is realized in inverse proportion to the frequency and ferocity with which debate is entered into. On the other hand, because in dialogue each partner comes with the intention of learning and changing herself, one's partner in fact will also change. Thus the alleged goal of debate, and much more, is accomplished far more effectively by dialogue.

If we are indeed open to "learning, changing, and growing," as Swidler has alluded, "a change in our attitude" toward the other is required. How else are we to maximize learning and to achieve a stable, positive supervisor-supervisee relationship and some semblance of a meaningful relationship with congregants?

Hence, the Western student may find that his or her mind-set must be moderated to allow him or her to be open to (1) theological insight born of intercultural dialogue, (2) a broader understanding of the mission of the church at home and abroad, (3) an increased sense of global awareness and cultural sensitivity, and (4) insight into ways of approaching ministry within an increasingly multicultural world. In light of these elements, consider Swidler's opening and closing statements in his third commandment: "Each participant must come to the dialogue with complete honesty and sincerity. No false fronts have any place in dialogue." This is what it takes to climb higher on the ladder toward the platform to engage in ministry, ministry that has the potential to make a difference.

I recommend reading Swidler's commandments in their entirety, as they are rich with the essentials for meaningful and effective dialogue. Do this as a small step toward dispelling the presupposition held among citizens of some countries—perhaps the one in which you desire to serve—that North Americans think that they know what's best for other nations and are only interested in monologue.

Swidler's commandments and the importance of the supervisor-supervisee and supervisee-congregation relationships are best demonstrated by an example. The Association Mwana Ukundwa (AMU), translated "Beloved Child Association," is a nongovernment organization in Rwanda, Africa. The Reverend Byiringiro Samuel, who serves as the field education supervisor, is the director and coordinator of the Evangelism Department. He considers one of the most important aspects of the placement to be students getting to know the stories of the people, which take into consideration their history and that of Rwanda. Demonstrating a genuine interest in congregants' stories will give you the best view of the intricacies of the task you are about to perform. Your sincere devotion to this simple act will afford you insight into a very complex society, one with a very bloody history of tribal rivalry. But it must be a dialogue. Therefore the Reverend Samuel asks students to share their stories as well, including pictures from home. When engaging in these dialogues, you should know your limitations and be self-aware, keeping in mind the power and the limits of your role.

A brief description of the Beloved Child Association's accomplishments—the platform—brings up the lights and sets the stage for students' purpose and ministry—the high wire. Here is a litany of those accomplishments in the Reverend Samuel's words.

> We have been working with more than 45 churches in the program called integral missions. Support more than 976 students in primary and high schools by providing material as schools' fees. Provide vocational training to 100 young people. Work with 20 schools in line of prevention HIV/AIDS and sexual violence. Support more than 300 children and parents who are HIV/AIDS positive. Support 40 groups of parents in income generating activities. Promote the culture of reading by providing 3 children's libraries in 3 provinces. Support different groups of traditional dancing and drumming as sport teams. Hosting different intercultural programs where young people and college students come over from Norway.

Every year students have participated in these and similar efforts, as they sought to make a difference.

Making a difference in ministry requires a dialogue whose primary purpose, as described by Swidler, is "to change and grow in the perception and understanding of reality and then to act accordingly." Such a dialogue will increase your capacity to be effective and minimize chances for error as you fulfill your ministry responsibilities. In addition, your supervisor will hold you in higher regard, believing that your interest in the placement is more than a means to an academic end. Thus a burgeoning relationship among the two of you, the congregation, and other constituents has a greater potential to take root. Balance makes all the difference if you hope to succeed, whatever that might mean to you. A dialogue characterized by humility, respect, curiosity, listening, and patience will go a long way toward constituting the platform that leads to ministry.

Let's describe in more detail what this supervisor-supervisee relationship should resemble, since it is so important to you and the placement. After all, you're going out on a high wire/ministry in an unfamiliar culture to face so many unknowns. One unknown is the net beneath you, your supervisor, whom you will first meet when you arrive. But who else is there to trust in a new place? Trust is a good place to start since you're stepping out onto a high wire. However, the supervisor knows that if this is to be a learning experience, he or she has to be willing to allow you to demonstrate leadership potential; he or she must trust you as well. Remember, the supervisor doesn't really know you, either. Taking risks becomes a factor in this newfound transcontinental relationship. How interesting: two strangers from very different cultures out on a high wire/in ministry together, performing an act, and trusting in God that the other will remember the many steps required. How do you say "faith?"

You might be worried about making an assumption that could lead to a sociocultural misstep, resulting in a spill sending you plunging into the net below and resulting in a bad bruise. Only remember, you will fall on the supervisor, the net. So think twice about the analogies and examples you use in sermons, while teaching and engaging in theological reflection with peers, and in everyday interactions. That's why it's so important that you put in time developing or enhancing your intercultural competence before arriving on site.

Could fear be the primary factor that leads to spills? Maybe the complexity of the unknowns became overwhelming. If so, I recommend a more collaborative effort between you and the supervisor. Perhaps he or she could be more supportive by guiding you through the steps as you get a handle on your fears and uncertainties. Yes, everything will be rather different and cultural clues not so obvious, but remember to be inquisitive. Ask a lot of questions! Your supervisor expects it, and it goes a long way toward dispelling fear of the unknown.

Consider asking the following questions as a starting point to equipping yourself for an international field education placement:

1. Will I receive a general orientation, including enhancing my cultural awareness?
2. Do you provide a support committee to assist with the educational process and transition into the life of the congregation?
3. Will my responsibilities be well defined and expectations outlined from the beginning? Or will I be expected to demonstrate eager curiosity and practice intuitive leadership?
4. What are some of the particular roles—family-related, work, social, and religious—in your culture that are gender specific?
5. Share with me what's considered appropriate dress on Sunday and for carrying out ministry responsibilities throughout the week.
6. What should I do, when, not if, I take a cultural misstep?
7. How do I wade through the waters of social behavioral tensions without causing a wake?
8. Offer your best advice on how I should relate to people, both congregants and those of the immediate and broader communities.
9. What type of courses do you recommend students take before arriving on site?
10. What are some general house rules when living with a host family?
11. Briefly describe some customs and religious practices and beliefs that I should be aware of before I arrive.
12. Tell me how to demonstrate respect toward authority figures. For example, are there formal and informal ways of addressing them?
13. What rituals and celebrations should I abstain from participating in while there?
14. What are some of the most important culture-related dates/historical events?

Like performing in a high-wire act, engaging in international field education can be thrilling, challenging, and inspiring. Prepare well, and pray for courage, wisdom, and strength. God will meet you there.

SUGGESTED READING

Armstrong, Richard Stoll, and Kirk Walker Morledge. *Help! I'm a Pastor: A Guide to Parish Ministry*. Louisville, KY: Westminster John Knox Press, 2005.

Deardorff, Darla, ed. *The SAGE Handbook of Intercultural Competence*. Thousand Oaks, CA: SAGE Publications, 2009.

Swidler, Leonard. "The Dialogue Decalogue: Ground Rules for Interreligious Dialogue." *Journal of Ecumenical Studies* 20, no. 1 (Winter 1983): 1–4.

Notes

FOREWORD

1. Christian A. B. Scharen and Eileen R. Campbell-Reed, "Learning Pastoral Imagination: A Five-Year Report on How New Ministers Learn in Practice," *Auburn Studies* (2016): 20, http://www.pastoralimagination.com (accessed October 12, 2016).

2. Dorothy Bass, Kathleen A. Cahalan, Bonnie J. Miller-Mclemore, James R. Nieman, and Christian B. Scharen, *Christian Practical Wisdom: What It Is, Why It Matters* (Grand Rapids, MI: Eerdmans, 2016), i.

3. Fortunately, new studies and new books are calling us to account for pedagogical practices that will best equip students to succeed as twenty-first-century pastors in the church and world. In addition to the study cited in note 1, the Association of Theological Schools has undertaken a study—its largest ever—into educational models for theological education. Daniel Aleshire, ATS Biennial Meeting address, 2016.

INTRODUCTION

1. Dorothy Bass, Kathleen A. Cahalan, Bonnie J. Miller-Mclemore, James R. Nieman, and Christian B. Scharen, *Christian Practical Wisdom: What It Is, Why It Matters* (Grand Rapids, MI: Eerdmans, 2016), 2–3.

1. ENGAGING THEOLOGICAL FIELD EDUCATION

1. I published a chapter on a related topic in *Welcome to Theological Field Education!* (Herndon, VA: The Alban Institute, 2011), and it has been significantly revised and updated here.

2. Charles R. Feilding, "Education for Ministry," *Theological Education* 3, no. 1 (Autumn 1966): 1–252.

3. Feilding, "Education for Ministry," 13.

4. Feilding, "Education for Ministry," 223.

5. Erik Erikson, *Identity and the Life Cycle* (New York: Norton, 1980); see chart on p. 129.

6. Parker J. Palmer, *Let Your Life Speak* (San Francisco: Jossey-Bass, 2000), 11.

7. Edward Cell, "Mapping Experiences," in *Learning to Learn from Experience* (Albany: State University of New York Press, 1984), ch. 3.

8. Eduard Lindeman, *The Meaning of Adult Education* (Montreal: Harvest House, 1961), 6.

9. S. Joseph Levine, *Getting to the Core: Reflections on Teaching and Learning* (Okemos, MI: LearnerAssociates.net, 2005), 101–102.

10. Donald A. Schon, *Educating the Reflective Practitioner* (San Francisco: Jossey-Bass, 1987), 22–40.

11. Schon, *Educating the Reflective Practitioner*, 103.

12. A good introduction through reflection on actual ministerial cases is found in Barbara Blodgett and Matthew Floding, eds., *Brimming with God* (Eugene, OR: Pickwick Publications, 2015).

13. Matthew Floding, "Fostering a Mentoring Environment," *Reflective Practice* 32 (2012): 272–281.

14. Godspace, "The Prayer of St. Brendan," March 19, 2014, http://godspace-msa.com/2014/03/19/the-prayer-of-st-brendan/ (accessed April 19, 2016).

2. ENGAGING WITH YOUR SUPERVISOR-MENTOR

1. Personal pronouns alternate between masculine and feminine throughout the chapter to improve readability.

2. Malcolm Knowles, *The Adult Learner: A Neglected Species*, 3rd ed. (Houston, TX: Gulf Publishing, 1984), 55–61. See also "The Adult Learning Theory—Andragogy—of Malcolm Knowles," eLearning Industry, http://elearningindustry.com/the-adult-learning-theory-andragogy-of-malcolm-knowles (accessed April 5, 2016).

3. Seminaries and divinity schools have different names for this formal learning agreement.

4. Matthew Floding, "Fostering a Mentoring Environment," *Reflective Practice* 32 (2013): 272–281.

5. Jane Vella, *Learning to Listen, Learning to Teach: The Power of Dialogue in Educating Adults* (San Francisco: Jossey-Bass, 1994), 3–22.

6. P. M. Forni, *Choosing Civility: The Twenty-five Rules of Considerate Conduct* (New York: St. Martin's Press, 2002), 44.

7. Étienne Wenger, Richard McDermott, and William Snyder, *Cultivating Communities of Practice: A Guide to Managing Knowledge* (Boston: Harvard Business School Press, 2002), 4.

8. Jean Lave and Étienne Wenger, *Situated Learning: Legitimate Peripheral Participation* (New York: Cambridge University Press, 1991), 53.

9. Matthew Floding and Glenn Swier, "Legitimate Peripheral Participation: Entering a Community of Practice," *Reflective Practice* 31 (2012): 193–204.

10. Matthew Floding, ed., *Welcome to Theological Field Education!* (Herndon, VA: Alban, 2011), 6.

11. Brené Brown explores how the courage to be vulnerable can be transformative in *Daring Greatly* (New York: Avery, 2012).

12. Craig Dykstra, "Pastoral and Ecclesial Imagination," in *For Life Abundant: Practical Theology, Theological Education, and Christian Ministry*, ed. Dorothy C. Bass and Craig Dykstra (Grand Rapids, MI: Eerdmans, 2008), 51.

13. Matthew Floding and Deborah Davis, "The Gift of One Hour," *Reflective Practice* 35 (2016): 197–214.

14. Barbara Blodgett addresses this in her helpful chapter "Are You Daniel or King Belshezzar? Soliciting Feedback Instead of Praise," in *Becoming the Pastor You Hope to Be: Four Practices for Improving Ministry* (Herndon, VA: Alban, 2011).

3. ENGAGING WITH YOUR
FIELD EDUCATION STUDENT

1. I published a chapter on a related topic in *Welcome to Theological Field Education!*, and it has been significantly revised and updated here.

2. Michael Pollan, *The Botany of Desire* (New York: Random House, 2001), 10.

3. George Hunter, *Theological Field Education* (Newton Centre, MA: Boston Theological Institute, 1977), 1.

4. In-service training conducted at Western Theological Seminary on February 2, 2010, by Dr. Charlene Jin Lee.

5. Amy Gostkowski, "What Makes a Great Coach?," *USA Hockey*, October 2009, 36.

6. Max DePree, *Leadership Jazz* (New York: Doubleday, 1992), 102–103.

7. Most field education programs will invite you to share the responsibility for mentoring your student with a lay mentoring team or committee. This affirms the people of God's active role in mentoring for ministry. Besides, laypersons have gifts and strengths to share that we don't have. This affirms Paul's use of the body metaphor. You can learn more about this potent team's work at Matthew Floding, "Fostering a Mentoring Environment," *Reflective Practice* 32 (n.d.): 272–282, http://journals.sfu.ca/rpfs/index.php/rpfs/article/view/77 (accessed July 20, 2016).

8. Survey conducted among summer 2015 field education participants at Duke Divinity School.

9. Lee Knefelkamp, Carole Widick, and Clyde A. Parker, guest editors, "Erik Erikson and Psychosocial Development," in *New Directions for Student Services: Applying New Developmental Findings* (San Francisco: Jossey-Bass, 1978), 6–7.

10. Donald A. Schon, *Educating the Reflective Practitioner* (San Francisco: Jossey-Bass, 1987), 163.

11. *Becoming a Pastor: Reflections on the Transition into Ministry* (Herndon, VA: Alban Institute, 2008), 13.

12. *Becoming a Pastor*, 14.

13. *Becoming a Pastor*, 30.

14. *Becoming a Pastor*, 39.

15. John E. Paver, *Theological Reflection and Education for Ministry: Explorations in Practical, Pastoral and Empirical Theology* (Burlington, VT: Ashgate Publishing, 2006), 3.

4. ENGAGING YOUR CONTEXT FOR MINISTRY

1. Some of you may be continuing in a field education setting that you know well because you began serving the congregation prior to entering seminary. You have the advantage of knowing some things about the context where you serve, but depending on how long you have served there, you may also carry the disadvantage of accepting the default interpretations of a place and no longer seeing truly what is around you and your congregation. If that is the case, this chapter encourages you to remember what it was like to enter this setting and to look upon it now with fresh eyes.

2. Wendell Berry, *Standing by Words: Essays* (San Francisco: North Point Press, 1983), 70.

3. For a more detailed description of these four approaches, see my book *Finding Voice: How Theological Field Education Shapes Pastoral Identity* (Eugene, OR: Wipf and Stock, 2012), ch. 2 and app. A. For an excellent discussion on understanding community shifts and patterns, see Rick Morse, *From Our Doorsteps: Developing a Ministry Plan That Makes Sense* (St. Louis, MO: Chalice Press, 2010), intro. and ch. 2.

5. ENGAGING IN MINISTRY ETHICALLY

1. See Office for Civil Rights, "Sexual Harassment: It's Not Academic," US Department of Education, http://www2.ed.gov/about/offices/list/ocr/docs/ocrshpam.html (accessed July 15, 2016).

2. See US Equal Employment Opportunity Commission, "Sexual Harassment," https://www.eeoc.gov/laws/types/sexual_harassment.cfm (accessed July 15, 2016).

6. ENGAGING IN THEOLOGICAL REFLECTION

1. From the plaque of literally the oldest pulpit in America, which graces the sanctuary of First Church in Albany, New York.

2. You can explore this more fully in the introductory chapter to *Brimming with God: Reflecting Theologically on Cases in Ministry*, ed. Barbara Blodgett and Matthew Floding (Eugene, OR: Pickwick Publications, 2015).

3. The Sustaining Pastoral Excellence Peer Learning Project has documented this in *So Much Better: How Thousands of Pastors Help Each Other Thrive* (St. Louis, MO: Chalice Press, 2013).

4. Matthew Floding and Deborah K. Davis, "The Gift of One Hour: Strategies for Reflective Supervision," *Reflective Practice* 36 (2016): 197–214.

5. In *Brimming with God*, eleven cases in ministry are reflected upon by twenty-three field educators modeling the application of a variety of theological reflection methods.

6. This pattern calls to mind Cardinal Joseph Cardijn's "See, Judge, Act," which was adapted for use by a number of communities throughout the world. Fr. Hugh O'Sullivan, chaplain to the Australian Young Christian Workers, developed nine questions to go with each: *See*, What exactly is happening? What is this doing to people? Why is this happening? *Judge*, What do you think about all this? What do you think should be happening? What does your faith say? *Act*, What exactly is it that you want to change? What action are you going to take now? Who can you involve in your action? Michael De La Bedoyere, *The Cardijn Story: A Study of the Life of Mgr. Joseph Cardijn and the Young Christian Workers' Movement* (London: Longmans Green, 1958).

7. For an expansion of this reflection and more examples, see Barbara Blodgett and Matthew Floding, "The Role of Theological Reflection within Field Education," *Reflective Practice* 34 (2014): 268–283.

8. Names and details have been altered to preserve confidentiality. There are Friendship Houses in Durham, NC; Holland, MI; and Nashville, TN, associated with Duke Divinity School, Western Theological Seminary, and Vanderbilt Divinity School, respectively.

9. From the newsletter of Blacknall Memorial Presbyterian Church and shared by the Rev. Allan Poole in May 2016 in personal conversation at our favorite coffee shop in Durham. Words of Institution have been inserted in italics between the man's statements.

7. ENGAGING IN SUSTAINING SPIRITUAL PRACTICES

1. Thomas Kelly, *A Testament of Devotion* (New York: Walker, 1987), 83.

2. Kelly, *Testament of Devotion*, 83.

3. Brian Taylor, *Spirituality for Everyday Living* (Collegeville, MN: Liturgical Press, 1989), 12.

4. Taylor, *Spirituality for Everyday Living*, 12.

5. Taylor, *Spirituality for Everyday Living*, 12.
6. Taylor, *Spirituality for Everyday Living*, 12.
7. Deborah Hunsinger, *Pray Without Ceasing* (Grand Rapids, MI: Eerdmans, 2006), xiv, 99–189.
8. Hunsinger, *Pray Without Ceasing*, 45–47.
9. Dan Wakefield. *The Story of Your Life: Writing a Spiritual Autobiography* (Boston: Beacon Press, 1990).
10. Margaret Guenther, *Holy Listening* (Cambridge, MA: Crowley Publications, 1992).
11. Brother Lawrence, *Practice of the Presence of God* (New York: Doubleday, 1977).
12. Julia Cameron, *The Artist's Way* (New York: Jeremy P. Tarcher/Putnam, 2002).

8. ENGAGING IN PERSONAL SELF-CARE

1. Luke 10:27.
2. H. R. Barton, "How Is It with Your Soul? Paying Attention to What Matters," *Christianity Today* (March 2010), http://www.christianitytoday.com/le/2010/march-online-only/how-is-it-with-your-soul.html (accessed July 2016).

10. ENGAGING THE LITURGICAL ARTS

1. I am led to believe that everyone is "called" to do something, whether that is to work in medicine, advocacy, fashion design, and so forth.
2. Because I experienced such a drastic transformation, a part of my teaching ministry has been to consult with dancers to help them discover or rediscover themselves as artists with purpose. Josetta Hoover, "Liturgical Dance as Transformative Worship: Meeting God through Movement" (DMin thesis, Wesley Theological Seminary, 2015).
3. Stephanie Butler, *My Body Is the Temple: Encounters and Revelations of Sacred Dance and Artistry* (Fairfax, VA: Xulon Press, 2001). This book has been used as a manual for dance ministries and liturgical arts for several years. An ordained elder in the African Methodist Episcopal Church, Rev. Butler has dedicated her life to preparing dance ministers and anyone who engages the liturgical arts for ministry.
4. With guidance from Richard Foster's *Celebration of Discipline*, I have introduced dancers to the inward and outward disciplines he discusses at length. With two of the dance ministries I worked with, we attempted to pray and fast corporately one day per week from 9:00 am to 5:00 pm. Essentially, we were to forgo our lunch meal and pray for one another during this time. A short devotional was sent out weekly to keep us focused.
5. This affirmation also addresses the cost of ministry, its inconvenience, and its discomfort. In the language of the Black Church Tradition, the anointing of the Holy Spirit is costly in relation to ministry.

12. ENGAGING IN EVANGELISM

1. For a powerful counterargument, see Paul J. Griffiths, *An Apology for Apologetics: A Study in the Logic of Interreligious Dialogue* (Maryknoll, NY: Orbis, 1991).
2. *Penn Says*, "A Gift of a Bible," episode 192, December 9, 2008.
3. See Howard Gardner, *Changing Minds: The Art and Science of Changing Our Own and Other People's Minds* (New York: Harvard Business School Press, 2004); Daniel Kahneman, *Thinking Fast and Slow* (New York: Farrar, Straus & Giroux, 2011); and John G. Stackhouse

Jr., *Need to Know: Vocation as the Heart of Christian Epistemology* (New York and Oxford: Oxford University Press, 2014).

4. For a bracing example, see Francis Spufford, *Unapologetic: Why, Despite Everything, Christianity Can Still Make Surprising Emotional Sense* (San Francisco: HarperOne, 2012).

13. ENGAGING IN FAITH FORMATION

1. Sunday school is chosen here as an example of a faith formation issue that you might face as you engage the dynamics of your theological field education setting.

2. Smokie Norful, "I Need You Now," 2002, EMI Gospel, *I Need You Now*.

3. Phil Vassar, "Good Ole Days," 2004, BMG Music, *Shaken, Not Stirred*.

4. Even Southern Baptist Church growth strategist Ken Hamphill assures his readers that he is "not arguing for a return to the 'good ole days' when he argues that Sunday school has the potential to revitalize American congregations. Ken Hamphill, *Revitalizing the Sunday Morning Dinosaur: A Sunday School Growth Strategy for the 21st Century* (Nashville, TN: Broadman & Holman, 1996), 24.

5. Ken Ham and Britt Beemer, *Already Gone: Why Your Kids Will Quit Church and What You Can Do to Stop It* (Green Forest, AR: Master Books, 2009). Notably, this statistical study concludes with regard to disengagement that even those who are now physically attending Sunday school week after week are in fact *already gone*.

6. John Cozy, "Learning without Questioning in America: The Sunday School Syndrome," Global Research (Center for Research on Globalization), http://www.globalresearch.ca/learning-without-questioning-in-america-the-sunday-school-syndrome/5364233 (accessed July 11, 2016).

7. Peter C. Hodgson, *God's Wisdom: Toward a Theology of Education* (Louisville, KY: Westminster John Knox, 1999), 125.

8. Mary Elizabeth Moore, *Teaching as a Sacramental Act* (Cleveland, OH: Pilgrim Press, 2004), 56 (emphasis in original).

9. Richard Robert Osmer, *The Teaching Ministry of Congregations* (Louisville, KY: Westminster John Knox, 2005), 27.

10. Charles R. Foster, Lisa E. Dahill, Lawrence A. Golemon, and Barbara Wang Tolentino, *Educating Clergy: Teaching Practices and Pastoral Imagination* (San Francisco: Jossey-Bass, 2005), 128.

11. Stephen B. Bevans, "What Has Contextual Theology to Offer the Church of the Twenty-First Century?," in *Contextual Theology for the Twenty-First Century*, ed. Stephen B. Bevans and Katalina Tahaafe-Williams (Eugene, OR: Pickwick Publications, 2011), 17 (emphasis in original).

12. Norma Cook Everist, *The Church as Learning Community: A Comprehensive Guide to Christian Education* (Nashville, TN: Abingdon, 2002), 106.

13. John Roberto, *Reimagining Faith Formation for the 21st Century: Engaging All Ages and Generations* (Naugatuck, CT: Lifelong Faith Associates, 2015).

14. Boyung Lee, *Transforming Congregations through Community: Faith Formation from the Seminary to the Church* (Louisville, KY: Westminster John Knox, 2013), 44, 52.

15. Maria Harris, *Fashion Me a People: Curriculum in the Church* (Louisville, KY: Westminster John Knox, 1989), 47: "The church does not *have* an educational program; it *is* an educational program" (emphasis in original); Charles Foster, *Educating Congregations: The Future of Christian Education* (Nashville, TN: Abingdon, 1994), 8: "I propose that instead of new educational program, we take seriously learning how to participate in *the formative and transformative events* of the Christian tradition and witness" (emphasis added).

16. United Church of Christ, "Faith Formation and Christian Education," http://www.ucc.org/education (accessed July 11, 2016) (emphasis added).

17. Hodgson, *God's Wisdom*, 125–126.

18. William R. DeLong, *Courageous Conversations: The Teaching and Learning of Pastoral Supervision* (Lanham, MD: University Press of America, 2009), 79.

19. Brother Lawrence, *The Practice of the Presence of God* (Grand Rapids, MI: Baker Books, 1967), preface.

20. Dietrich Bonhoeffer, *Life Together*, trans. John W. Doberstein (New York: Harper & Row, 1954), 97.

21. Lee, *Transforming Congregations through Community*, 75–105; Eric H. F. Law, *The Wolf Shall Dwell with the Lamb: A Spirituality for Leadership in a Multicultural Community* (St. Louis, MO: Chalice Press, 1993), 121–131.

22. Craig Dykstra, "A Way of Seeing: Imagination and the Pastoral Life," *Christian Century* (April 8, 2008): 26.

23. Foster, Dahill, Golemon, and Tolentino, *Educating Clergy*, 24, 7.

14. ENGAGING IN CHURCH ADMINISTRATION

1. In the United Methodist Church elders are authorized to preach and teach the Word, to provide pastoral care and counsel, to administer the sacraments, and *to order the life of the church* for service in mission and ministry as pastors, superintendents, and bishops. Book of Discipline, http://www.umc.org/what-we-believe/para-340-responsibilities-and-duties-of-elders-and-licensed-pastors (accessed June 2, 2016). Ministerial leaders in other traditions will use similar language appropriate to their polity. Learn the vocabulary of your tradition!

15. ENGAGING FOR FAITHFUL LEADERSHIP

1. Travis Bradberry and Jean Greaves, *Emotional Intelligence 2.0* (San Diego, CA: Talent-Smart, 2009).

2. James Kouzes and Barry Posner, *The Leadership Challenge* (San Francisco: Jossey-Bass, 2002). Kouzes and Posner provide a research-based explanation of the five practices essential to organizational leadership: Model the Way, Inspire a Shared Vision, Challenge the Process, Enable Others to Act, and Encourage the Heart.

3. Tom Rath and Barry Conchie, *Strengths Based Leadership: Great Leaders, Teams and Why People Follow* (New York: Gallup Press, 2008).

4. Jim Collins, *Good to Great* (New York: HarperBusiness, 2001).

5. Ronald Heifetz, Alexander Grashow, and Martin Linsky, *Practice of Adaptive Leadership* (Boston: Harvard Business Press, 2009).

6. Peter Senge, *The Fifth Discipline: The Art and Practice of the Learning Organization* (New York: Doubleday, 1990).

7. See Thomas Merton, *New Seeds of Contemplation* (New York: New Directions, 1961). There are multiple texts on contemplation as a Christian practice, and leadership literature is increasingly interested in mindfulness, albeit as a quasi-religious practice. Contemplation, here, is particularly Christian and pursues communion with God for the sake of loving the world. Other writings on contemplation include *The Interior Castle* (Avila), *The Imitation of Christ* (Kempis), and *Pensées* (Pascal), among others.

8. Douglas Stone and Sheila Heen, *Thanks for the Feedback: The Science and Art of Receiving Feedback Well* (New York: Viking, 2014), 8.

9. Creating pull is "mastering the skills required to drive our own learning; it's about how to recognize and manage our resistance, how to engage in feedback conversations with confidence and curiosity, and even when the feedback seems wrong, how to find insight that might help us grow." Stone and Heen, *Thanks for the Feedback*, 6.

10. Each of the three types of feedback has a different purpose. Learning leaders ask different questions depending on what type of feedback and what type of learning they desire. They ask for *appreciation* when they desire solidarity and belonging. Appreciative feedback seeks gratitude, motivation, connection, and acknowledgment. They ask for *coaching* in order to

expand knowledge, sharpen skills, or improve capability. Coaching feedback invites transformation according to the mentor/intern's shared expectations. They ask for *evaluation* to rate or rank against a standard, namely a mentor's or community's expectations. Evaluation exists to align expectations and to inform decision making. Evaluation is the most feared yet least offered form of feedback, in that standards need to be clearly defined in order for evaluative feedback to be most helpful. Stone and Heen, *Thanks for the Feedback*, 29–35.

11. Stone and Heen, *Thanks for the Feedback*, 183–204.

12. Wesley Granberg Michaelson, *Unexpected Destinations: An Evangelical Pilgrimage to World Christianity* (Grand Rapids, MI: Eerdmans, 2011), 170.

16. ENGAGING IN PUBLIC MINISTRY

1. Curtiss Paul DeYoung, *Living Faith: How Faith Inspires Social Justice* (Minneapolis, MN: Fortress Press, 2007), Kindle e-book, loc. 132.

2. James M. Washington, ed., "Letter from a Birmingham City Jail," *A Testament of Hope* (San Francisco: HarperSanFrancisco, 1986), 290.

3. Joe Holland and Peter Henriot, *Social Analysis: Linking Faith and Justice* (Washington, DC: Center of Concern, 1983), 98–101.

4. Attributed to numerous systems thinkers. David P. Stroh, *Systems Thinking for Social Change: A Practical Guide to Solving Complex Problems, Avoiding Unintended Consequences, and Achieving Lasting Results* (White River Junction, VT: Chelsea Green Publishing, 2015).

5. Danielle L. Ayers and Reginald W. Williams Jr., *To Serve This Present Age: Social Justice Ministries in the Black Church* (Valley Forge, PA: Judson Press, 2013), 6.

6. Allan Hugh Cole Jr., *A Spiritual Life: Perspectives from Poets, Prophets, and Preachers* (Louisville, KY: Westminster John Knox Press, 2011), 232–233.

18. ENGAGING AS A GENDERED PERSON

1. William L. Andrews, ed., *Sisters of the Spirit: Three Black Women's Autobiographies of the Nineteenth Century* (Bloomington: Indiana University Press, 1986), 36.

2. Ashley-Anne Masters and Stacy Smith, *Bless Her Heart: Life as a Young Clergy Woman* (St. Louis, MO: Chalice Press, 2011), 54.

3. James D. Whitehead and Evelyn Eaton Whitehead, "Transgender Lives: From Bewilderment to God's Extravagance," *Pastoral Psychology* 63 (2014): 171–184.

4. Jane Busey, "Is the Glass Ceiling Cracking?," *Connections* (Spring 2014): 8.

5. Analysis of the annual Bureau of Labor Statistics as quoted in "The Pay Gap at Church," *Christian Century* (February 17, 2016): 7.

6. Sally B. Purvis, *The Stained Glass Ceiling: Churches and Their Women Pastors* (Louisville, KY: Westminster John Knox Press, 1995), 100.

7. Carol Howard Merritt, "Church in the Making: Leading like Lydia," *Christian Century* (March 2, 2016): 45.

8. Masters and Smith, *Bless Her Heart*, vii.

19. ENGAGING RACE

1. Mark Chaves, The National Congregations Study, 20-21, http://www.soc.duke.edu/natcong/Docs/NCSIII_report_final.pdf (accessed October 12, 2016).

2. Fumitaka Matsuoka, *The Color of Faith: Building Community in a Multiracial Society* (Cleveland, OH: United Church Press, 1998), 95.

3. Grace Ji-Sun Kim, "Hybridity, Postcolonialism and Asian American Women," *Feminist Theology* 24, no. 3 (2016): 266.

4. Matsuoka, *Color of Faith*, 3.

5. As I write this, fourteen-year-old Royce Mann's slam poetry performance, "White Boy Privilege," acknowledging this reality, has reportedly gone viral. See Karen Yuan and Lucy Price, "Teen's 'White Boy Privilege' Slam Poetry Goes Viral," CNN, http://www.cnn.com/2016/07/13/us/teen-slam-poet-white-privilege-hln/ (accessed July 15, 2016).

6. See *Tim Wise: Anti-Racist Essayist, Author, and Educator*, http://www.timwise.org.

7. Arun Mukherjee, Alok Mukherjee, and Barbara Godard, "Translating Minoritized Cultures: Issues of Caste, Class and Gender," *Postcolonial Text* 2 (2006): 1.

8. John Solomos, "Beyond Racism and Multiculturalism," *Patterns of Prejudice* 32 (1998): 49.

20. ENGAGING IN A NONPROFIT CONTEXT

1. An excellent discussion of the role mission and vision statements play in the strategic planning of nonprofit organizations is found in Michael Allison and Jude Kaye, *Strategic Planning for Nonprofit Organizations: A Practical Guide for Dynamic Times* (Hoboken, NJ: John Wiley and Sons, 2015), 27–96.

2. There are many useful accounts of relationship-driven, broad-based community organizing. Kendall Clark Baker describes the process of building intentional public relationships in *When Faith Storms the Public Square: Mixing Religion and Politics through Community Organizing to Enhance Our Democracy* (Alresford, UK: Circle Books, 2011), 137–148. See also Edward Chambers, *Roots for Radicals: Organizing for Power, Action, and Justice* (New York: Bloomsbury Academic, 2014), 44–54.

3. Although her book focuses on congregational settings, Sarah Drummond describes a number of useful tools for designing programs that generate clear outcomes and assessment strategies for measuring them in *Holy Clarity: The Practice of Planning and Evaluation* (Herndon, VA: Alban Institute, 2009).

21. ENGAGING IN CLINICAL PASTORAL EDUCATION

1. The CPE I reference in this article is offered through the Association for Clinical Pastoral Education (ACPE), which is nationally recognized as an accrediting agency in the field of clinical pastoral education by the US Secretary of Education through the US Department of Education. Clinical pastoral education began in 1925 as a form of theological education that takes place not exclusively in academic classrooms, but also in clinical settings where ministry is being practiced. Association for Clinical Pastoral Education, "About Us," https://www.acpe.edu/ACPE/About_ACPE/ACPE/About_ACPE/About_ACPE.aspx?hkey=8bda1439-a609-475c-83ba-d86c9ca8e7e4 (accessed April 19, 2016).

2. A CPE supervisor is an individual who is ordained and endorsed or commissioned by his or her faith group and has undergone three to five years of postgraduate training to learn the art of CPE supervision. While in training, they are required to meet regularly with peers and certified ACPE-CPE supervisors to review their work. Having successfully written and received approval for their theory papers and met regional and national committees, the person is certified by ACPE to offer ACPE-CPE.

3. A verbatim is the written account of a pastoral conversation in which the writer recon-structs, to the best of his or her ability, what was spoken between the pastor and the congre-gant(s). Following the conversation, the writer will be asked to reflect upon the conversation through a variety of lenses, including theological, sociocultural, behavioral, and personal. Ano-nymity of persons is always expected.

4. Didactics are teaching moments focused on a particular topic, such as "Ministry to Persons at the Time of Death."

5. Antoin Boisen, known as the founder of the CPE movement, coined the phrase "living human document" to describe the encounter with the living person in which we not only learn about him or her, but in turn are able to learn more about ourselves, our relationships with others, and ultimately, our relationship with God.

6. Clinical pastoral education is also offered in retirement facilities, veterans' hospitals, hospices, and parish settings.

7. A chaplain is a minister who is assigned to provide religious and spiritual services within an institution. For further reading about chaplains and their work, I suggest Lawrence Holst, ed., *Hospital Ministry: The Role of the Chaplain Today* (New York: Crossroad Publish-ing, 2007).

8. A chaplain intern is a person enrolled in a CPE program for the first time and usually for one unit of CPE. One unit is granted after having completed four hundred hours of education and clinical work.

9. "Dry bones" is a reference to Ezekiel 37:1–14.

10. Ps. 23.

11. Alcoholics Anonymous, "Spiritual Experience," in *Alcoholics Anonymous* (New York: Alcoholics Anonymous World Services, 1939), 568.

12. Chaplain residents are typically individuals who enroll in a yearlong program of train-ing.

13. Reference to Acts 3:1–10.

22. ENGAGING TECHNOLOGY IN FIELD EDUCATION

1. Madeleine L'Engle, *Walking on Water* (Wheaton, IL: H. Shaw, 1980), 51.

23. ENGAGING MINISTRY IN SECULAR SETTINGS

1. The Pew Forum on Religion and Public Life, *"Nones" on the Rise: One-in-Five Adults Have No Religious Affiliation* (Washington, DC: Pew Research Center, 2012), http://www.pewforum.org/2012/10/09/nones-on-the-rise/.

2. Edgar H. Schein, *Humble Inquiry* (San Francisco: Berrett-Koehler Publishers, 2013).

3. Schein, *Humble Inquiry*.

4. ATFE 2013 Keynote speech by Patricia Killen. She emphasized that our job as field educators is to slow down the rush to judgment in our students and help them see the layers in any given situation.

5. Jennifer R. Ayers, *Waiting for a Glacier to Move: Practicing Social Witness* (Eugene, OR: Pickwick, 2011).

6. For example, see Melissa M. Kelley, *Grief: Contemporary Theory and the Practice of Ministry* (Minneapolis, MN: Fortress Press, 2010).

7. Gen. 2:22.

Index

advocacy, 68, 101, 102. *See also* social justice

boundaries, 31–32, 49, 66, 114. *See also* relationship(s)

children: and confidentiality, 30; and faith formation, 79–80; and suffering, 131
communication, 19, 106–107; through body language, 114–50; of expectations, 106; virtual vs. in-person, 136–137
confidentiality, 30, 49–51
context(s), 23–27; challenges of leading in a new, 24–25, 25–26; the importance of learning about your ministerial, 25, 53–54, 75–76, 80–81, 113, 125–126, 142–144, 148–149; ministry in nontraditional, 123–128, 141–146, 147–152
counsel, counseling, 68–69; and peer support, 49–50; receiving, 50–51. *See also* pastoral care; therapy, receiving clinical

difference(s), diversity: cultural, 148–149; embracing, 108–109, 121; generational, 105–109; racial, 119–121; sensitivity to, 114
discipleship: and evangelism, 73–74, 75–76; and faith formation, 80–81. *See also* faith formation

diversity. *See* difference(s), diversity

faith formation, 79–83; definition, 80–81; internship as opportunity for your, 6–10, 12–15, 19–21, 37–38, 92; process and programs, 81–83. *See also* discipleship
feedback: importance of receiving, 15–16, 56–57, 92–93, 94–95, 132–133; types, 159n10, 160n11
field education: history of, 6; spiritual growth as the goal of, 6–8

leaders, leadership: already in your setting, 107–108; cultivating, in your context, 87; developing, skills in your internship, 91–92; team approach to, 82–83

pastoral care, 65–72; and balancing with personal life, 65–67; in Clinical Pastoral Education (CPE) setting, 130–131; preparation for, 67; strategies for, 68–71

race, racism: in church, 120–121; definition, 118–119; different experiences of, 119–120; in your context, 98–101. *See also* difference(s), diversity

About the Contributors

Willard Walden Christopher Ashley, Sr., is the dean of the seminary and tenured associate professor of practical theology at the New Brunswick Theological Seminary. Reverend Ashley is also a psychoanalyst and served as the senior pastor at four different congregations over a thirty-two-year period. He envisioned and implemented the largest clergy resiliency program in the United States following the attacks on September 11, 2001, the Care for the Caregivers Interfaith Program, a ministry of the Council of Churches of the City of New York, funded by the American Red Cross and United Way. His ministry includes service as a consultant on disaster recovery and clergy self-care; vice president, Disaster Chaplaincy Services, New York City; board member, Northern New Jersey American Red Cross; former assistant dean of students, director of recruitment, and current board member, Andover Newton Theological School; and past president of the Blanton-Peale Graduate Institute, Alumni Association. Ashley is an ordained minister in the National Baptist Convention, USA, Inc., and the American Baptist Churches, USA.

Barbara J. Blodgett is assistant professor of pastoral leadership at Lexington Theological Seminary. She is a minister, educator, and ethicist. She formerly served as director of supervised ministries at Yale Divinity School. An ordained minister in the United Church of Christ, she has served in parish ministry as well as the national setting of the UCC in addition to field education. She has published three books: *Constructing the Erotic: Sexual Ethics and Adolescent Girls*; *Lives Entrusted: An Ethic of Trust for Ministry*; and *Becoming the Pastor You Hope to Be: Four Practices for Improving Ministry*. Blodgett received an MDiv from Yale Divinity School and a PhD from Yale University.

Jason Byassee serves in the Butler Chair in Homiletics and Biblical Interpretation at Vancouver School of Theology and is a fellow in theology and leadership at Duke Divinity School. He is the author, most recently, of *Trinity: The God We Don't Know* (Abingdon). Byassee is an elder in the United Methodist Church and previously supervised ministerial interns at Boone United Methodist Church in North Carolina. Byassee earned his MDiv at Duke Divinity School and PhD at Duke University.

Sung Hee Chang is assistant professor of Christian education and director of supervised ministry in Charlotte, NC, at Union Presbyterian Seminary. Previously Chang served as an educator for several churches in Virginia and North Carolina. Her areas of special interest include curriculum theory, with a particular focus on gender, race, identity, and postcolonial studies; intercultural theological education; ecumenical formation; interreligious education; and theological field education. She currently serves on the Presbyterian Church (PCUSA) Educator Certification Committee. She received her MACE and PhD from Union Presbyterian Seminary.

Kimberly L. Clayton is a minister of Word and Sacrament in the Presbyterian Church (PCUSA) and serves as the director of contextual education at Columbia Theological Seminary. She served as a pastor in churches for twenty-one years prior to working in theological education. Kim continues to preach and teach in congregations and at conferences. She is also a contributing writer to six volumes of liturgy for *Feasting on the Word: A Worship Companion* and essays in several volumes of *Feasting on the Word: Preaching the Revised Common Lectionary*; *Inclusive Marriage Services: A Wedding Sourcebook*; and *Brimming with God: Reflecting Theologically on Cases in Ministry*.

Deborah K. Davis is a Presbyterian minister (PCUSA) who earned her MDiv with a concentration in pastoral theology from Princeton Theological Seminary. She also received certification as a spiritual director from Oasis Ministries. She served as chaplain and director of the religious ministries at the University Medical Center at Princeton for twenty years and also as a nursing home chaplain and prison chaplain, before being called in 2007 to serve at her current position as the director of field education and administrative faculty of Princeton Theological Seminary. Davis has also served as moderator of the New Brunswick Presbytery and as a spiritual director.

Matthew Floding is director of ministerial formation at Duke Divinity School. A minister in the Reformed Church in America, he has served as pastor, college chaplain, and dean of students and director of field education at Western Theological Seminary (Holland, MI). Floding is a past chair of the steering committee of the Association for Theological Field Education and has contributed a number of articles addressing field education in the journal *Reflective Practice*. Floding is general editor of *Welcome to Theological Field Education!* and coeditor of *Brimming with God: Reflecting Theologically on Cases in Ministry*. He received his MDiv from McCormick Theological Seminary, MA in church history from Wheaton Graduate School, and DMin from Western Theological Seminary.

Susan E. Fox is the professor of supervised ministry and director of vocational planning at Union Presbyterian Seminary. A field educator since 1989, she is the coauthor of *Here I Am Lord: Now What?* and coeditor of and contributor to *Legal Issues in Theological Field Education*. An ordained minister in the Unitarian Universalist Association, she also currently serves as a community minister at the UU Community Church in Glen Allen, VA.

Josie Hoover is an adjunct professor of liturgical dance at Wesley Theological Seminary. Previously she served in the Practice in Ministry & Mission Program from 2007 to 2015 as a program administrator and assistant director. She has been involved in the liturgical arts since 2001, dancing with several ministries in the Washington, DC, area. An avid lover of dance, Josie currently serves as a company member and chaplain for Dancing by the Power: Movement Matters, Inc., a sacred arts dance company located in Adelphi, MD. She earned her MDiv and DMin at Wesley Theological Seminary.

Lucinda Huffaker is director of supervised ministries at Yale Divinity School and executive secretary of the Religious Education Association. Prior to holding her present position at Yale, Lucinda was associate director and then director of the Wabash Center for Teaching and Learning in Theology and Religion.

Grace Ji-Sun Kim is an associate professor of theology at Earlham School of Religion. She is the author or editor of ten books, most recently *Embracing the Other* (Eerdmans, 2016) and *Here I Am* (Judson Press, 2016). She is a book series editor at Palgrave Macmillan for the series Asian Christianity in the Diaspora. Kim received her MDiv from Knox College (University of Toronto) and her PhD from the University of Toronto. She is an ordained minister in the Presbyterian Church (PCUSA).

William B. Kincaid is the Herald B. Monroe Associate Professor of Leadership and Ministry Studies at Christian Theological Seminary. From 2008 to 2014 he served as director of field education at CTS, and from July 2014 to

June 2016 he served as interim vice president for academic affairs and dean of the faculty. He is the author of *Finding Voice: How Theological Field Education Shapes Pastoral Identity*. Along with MDiv and DMin from Lexington Theological Seminary, Kincaid also holds an MS in higher education from the University of Kentucky.

Nathan E. Kirkpatrick is the managing director of Alban at Duke Divinity School and one of the managing directors of leadership education at Duke Divinity. An Episcopal priest, he spends most of his time teaching and learning from clergy and congregational, denominational, and institutional leaders around the United States and the world. He holds degrees from Wake Forest University and Duke University and is a doctoral candidate at the University of Durham (UK).

W. Joseph Mann is adjunct professor of parish work at Duke Divinity School. For twenty-seven years he has taught courses on leadership in rural and small membership churches. He has served as a parish minister in Wilmington, NC, and as a campus minister at North Carolina State University. He was director of continuing education at Duke Divinity School from 1984 to 1989. For twenty years he was a director at the Duke Endowment. He returned to Duke Divinity School in 2009 and was a director for leadership education at Duke Divinity. He currently chairs the Field Education Committee at Duke and helps supervise area Field Education Reflection Groups. He has worked extensively in the nonprofit world, chairing the NC Center for Nonprofits, Duke's Center for Documentary Studies, and the Methodist Home for Children. He serves on the NC Annual Conference's Board of Ordained Ministry.

James Marshall, MA, has been a practicing clinical psychotherapist for twenty-nine years, specializing in the treatment of traumatic stress and relationships. He is currently the chair/CEO of the 911 Wellness Foundation and educates emergency responders in personal resilience and management of high-risk calls involving mental illness and suicide. Jim received his MA in clinical psychology from Wheaton College Graduate School.

Chester Polk is an associate director of field education at Princeton Theological Seminary. An ordained minister in the American Baptist Church, he directs the International Program at Princeton Theological Seminary. He has served as a pastor, home missionary, vice moderator of the Western District Association of Churches, two terms on the steering committee of the Association for Theological Field Education, two terms on the board of the Association of Ministry Guidance Professionals, and two terms as chair of the Association of Ministry Guidance Professionals. He earned his DMin at Princeton Theological Seminary.

Jim Rawlings, Jr., is director of pastoral services at Duke University Hospital in Durham, NC. He is an ordained elder in the United Methodist Church of the North Carolina Conference, a certified supervisor in the Association for Clinical Pastoral Education, a certified fellow in the American Association of Pastoral Counselors, and member of the North Carolina Chaplains' Association. Jim received his BA from Western Illinois University, his MDiv and ThM from Duke Divinity School, and his DMin from Princeton Theological Seminary.

John E. Senior is the director of the Art of Ministry Program at the Wake Forest University School of Divinity and assistant teaching professor of ethics and society. Senior is the author of *A Theology of Political Vocation: Christian Life and Public Office* and a teaching elder in the Presbyterian Church (PCUSA). He earned his MDiv from Harvard Divinity School and his PhD from Emory University.

Kyle J. A. Small is dean of formation for ministry and associate professor of church leadership at Western Theological Seminary in Holland, MI. He and his wife, Lindsay, served congregations in Chicago, Minneapolis, and southwestern Michigan. His life as pastor and teacher finds resonance when he explores the church as a socio-theological community. Kyle's teaching and research focus on mission-shaped ecclesiology, spiritual formation, leading Christian communities, and theological education. He is published in the missional church series from Eerdmans and served on the editorial team for *Religious Leadership: A Reference Handbook*. Kyle has an MDiv from North Park Theological Seminary and a PhD in missiology from Luther Seminary.

John G. Stackhouse, Jr., holds the Samuel J. Mikolaski Chair of Religious Studies at Crandall University in Moncton, New Brunswick, where he also serves as dean of faculty development. He has engaged in public apologetics at many universities, including Harvard, Yale, and Stanford, and his commentary has been featured in the *New York Times*, the *Washington Post*, *Time*, ABC News, NBC News, and elsewhere. He is the author of ten books, including *Humble Apologetics: Defending the Faith Today*.

Laura S. Tuach is assistant director of field education and an instructor in ministry studies at Harvard Divinity School. She has served as chair and cochair of the Boston Theological Institute's Field Educators Consortium and on the steering committee of the Association for Theological Education. Prior to becoming a field educator she was the associate director of Partakers, a faith-based, nonprofit organization committed to reducing recidivism through education for incarcerated women and men. Tuach received her MDiv from Harvard Divinity School and is an ordained United Church of Christ (UCC) minister.

David W. Watkins, III, is the co-vocational pastor of Greater Bethesda Missionary Baptist Church and serves as the associate director of experiential education and field studies at McCormick Theological Seminary, both in Chicago. With a passion for leadership, church renewal, and community revitalization, David also serves in a leadership capacity on several boards/committees, including the American Baptist Churches of Metro Chicago and the Washington Park Consortium. David is happily married to his beautiful college sweetheart, Latasha, and they are the proud parents of two sons, Jadon and Jonathan.